FLORENCE NIGHTINGALE

FLORENCE NIGHTINGALE

Fictionalized Biography

by

Sandy Dengler

MOODY PRESS

CHICAGO

ISBN: 0-8024-2627-1

1 2 3 4 5 6 Printing/LC/Year 92 91 90 89 88

Printed in the United States of America

Contents

Preface

Dr. Samuel Gridley Howe studied the tall, slender girl across the table. "Miss Nightingale, your Aunt Hannah must be quite a Christian lady."

"Oh, she is, sir—a person to whom all unseen things seem real and eternal things are near. She awakened me to realities of the faith."

"And those realities are . . . ?"

"She showed me that you can be happy only if you are at one with God. The only way to have that union is to get rid of the sin that keeps you separated from God. And the only way to do that is to commit yourself to Jesus Christ, whose blood paid for your sin. Only after I've accepted Jesus Christ and have that oneness with God can I begin to look for happiness."

"And, Miss Nightingale, are you happy and content now?"

"No, Dr. Howe, I am not."

Florence Nightingale. She was born into the wealthiest social class of her time. She attended sparkling balls and parties. Heads of state were her personal friends. She saved thousands of lives. To millions, she became a true heroine. And yet of all her ninety years, very few were happy.

For Florence was born and raised in the England of Queen Victoria. Victorian English men and women had definite ideas about what a well-born lady should—and should not—do. And well-born ladies like Florence did *not* become nurses.

But that is what she thought God called her to do. It wasn't easy. It took her years to overcome the objections of her family. She refused three marriage proposals. She did things "proper" Victorian folk would never do. She lost her health. Still, she would not abandon the job God set for her.

And He used her mightily.

1

Honestly, Flo!

May 1842

A black nanny-goat rolled her big brown eyes and stood smack in the middle of the road. Her harness hung on her, much too big. The cart she pulled needed paint. The boy who drove her gripped the rope around her neck and dragged goat and cart together off to the side of the road.

The Nightingale carriage rattled past them, splashing mud.

Sister Parthe glanced disgustedly at the goat cart as they passed. She patted her brown hair and adjusted her bonnet. "Can you imagine that? He almost made us slow down. That ragamuffin with the goat."

"He lives down in Wellow on the back lane. His father died of typhus last winter. Now he helps support his mother by hauling produce in his cart." Florence sat beside Parthe in the soft leather seat. She folded her hands. She loved riding in the open carriage like this, with the breeze on her face. She enjoyed listening to the gentle, constant *plop-plop* as their horses trotted smartly up the road.

Parthe scowled. "You know all these lower class scamps by name. I should think you might apply your time and effort to meeting a few of the people in our own class. Honestly, Flo."

In the seat across from her, Papa snickered. "Parthe, your sister knows most everyone of our station, and I daresay she's met more than a few of the very highest class. Now stop your nattering. You'll spoil a perfectly lovely evening."

The Nightingale carriage rumbled up the familiar curving drive to the front door of Broadlands Manor. Somewhere inside the great house, a string quartet played. No, wait—it was a full chamber orchestra. Lord Palmerston never did things by halves.

Footmen helped delicate, lovely Mama from the carriage. Tall, lanky Papa stepped down and offered Mama his arm. Parthe took her time climbing out. She carefully arranged her skirts and hair. Finally she stepped out of the way so Flo could descend.

Bright lights and music filled the great house, as always when the Palmerstons had a party. The Nightingales were properly announced as they entered the doors. And now Flo was swept into the giddy hoopla.

And the war inside her rose to the surface again. She felt sorry for the girls who stood about waiting for a bit of attention. And yet she felt guilty about receiving so much of it herself. But that was not the half of her guilty feelings.

Here came Lord Palmerston himself, master of Broadlands. He shook hands with Papa. What a contrast between the two! Papa was built like a flagpole—when he wore his top hat, like a schooner mast. Lord Palmerston, though, was a roly-poly Father Christmas of a fellow, all jolly. Flo loved the way his muttonchop whiskers curled around his cheeks. They shifted every time he smiled.

He kissed Mama's hand. "Milady, lovely as ever."

He nodded to Parthe. "Parthenope, good evening."

And he grabbed Flo's hand and led her off. "There's someone you must meet. I've been talking you up."

Chandeliers glittered with a thousand candles. Dancers moved out onto the polished floor.

"Here we are. Florence, dear, this is Richard Monckton Milnes, a Yorkshireman presently residing on Pall Mall. His specialty is poetry and breakfast. Richard, Miss Florence Nightingale, the only young woman here with a wit quicker than yours. If you two will excuse me . . . ?" And instantly, Father Christmas with the moveable muttonchops disappeared.

"I hear you speak Italian, French, and German, and translate Greek and Latin." He bowed as she curtsied. "Why?"

"Because not all great thinkers speak English. Why poetry and breakfast?"

He laughed delightfully and long. "Henry's right —can't tip you off balance. Forgive my rudeness just now. I enjoy poetry—indeed, all good use of words—and I have this reputation for inviting people to breakfast. It's a particular pleasure of mine."

"I've heard of you!"

This man cut a dashing figure, too, with his fashionable wool coat, rich brocade waistcoat, and slim, tight trousers stretched over pointed boots.

Two days later, the Palmerstons visited the Nightingales, for Broadlands lay only a few miles from Embley Park, the Nightingales' winter home. Richard Monckton Milnes came, too. And again and again and again.

In July Flo and her family traveled north to their summer home at Lea Hurst. Rather like birds migrating, Flo thought; Lea Hurst in summer, London during the fall social season, Embley in winter, London again in spring. Somehow, Richard Monckton Milnes ended up at Lea Hurst, too. And he went with them to visit the Duke of Devonshire.

Flo had never before seen Chatsworth, the ancestral home of the Duke, although it was close to Lea Hurst. And though she and her family visited many estates, never had she seen anywhere else like Chatsworth. Mary queen of Scots had been imprisoned in its original mansion. The present mansion was new—only about two hundred years old.

But the glasshouse*—ah! The glasshouse fascinated Flo. The building covered over an acre. It was one giant room, one story high on each side and two stories tall in the middle. Steel rods, bent into curving arches, held shaped glass panes. The whole house. Glass. Amazing, this modern age!

Greenhouse.

Inside, palm trees spread their fronds high over-head. A jungle of other tropical plants filled the house. Gravel paths wound among them.

The duke was proud of his glasshouse. Tonight he featured a promenade there. The whole place was lighted with candles, lanterns, and lamps. Thousands of lights twinkled and glittered. They filled the glasshouse; it glowed like day. Their light spilled through the transparent walls into the gardens all around.

Flo stood a few moments to simply gape at the glory. Couples were strolling through the door. She should wait inside for Parthe, so they could walk together. She stepped inside, into warm, damp air. So this was the climate explorers and missionaries worked in.

Carefully, she touched a long, bright green leaf.

"Banana plant."

She jumped.

The man was a pleasant fellow, slight of build and very quick. He dipped his head. "Joseph Paxton at your service."

"Florence Nightingale. How do you do." Then the name clicked. "You're the Duke's head gardener, the man who built all this." She nodded toward the broad leaves. "Banana. Really!"

"Out in the wild, wind splits the leaves. Virtually shreds them. Here they're protected, so they stay in one piece. But they tear very easily, as you see." And he cheerfully ripped the nearest leaf! Flo gasped.

She began asking questions. Mr. Paxton answered them eagerly, as if he were glad someone noticed the rich variety of plants he so lovingly grew. They strolled the paths together, talking. Flo wished somehow all of England could be housed in glass like this. She so despised cold. It ate into her bones. This tropical warmth was heavenly.

Very near the end of their stroll, Flo met Parthe. She had forgotten all about her! Mr. Paxton kissed her knuckles, thanked her for the pleasant time, and hurried off to other duties.

"He looks a bit old for you, but I'm sure he's fascinating." Parthe's voice dripped ice.

"He's the man who built the glasshouse, the man in charge. I'm very sorry I didn't wait for you." Parthe was excellent at temper tantrums. Flo had better humor her.

"Honestly, Flo! You're a constant embarrassment to me! Poor Henry mooning over you, wanting to marry. You lead him on while you lead Monckton Milnes on. Now you're strolling with still another gentleman, and I'll bet he's married already!"

"Parthe, he was showing me the plantings. I don't—"

"And the way you're always groveling around playing nurse! It's disgusting. I'm ashamed to show my face—afraid someone will learn what you're doing. You make Mama and me so mad!"

"This is not the time or place to—" Flo glanced around.

Then the son of one of Mama's friends, Howard Somebody, came walking by. Parthe switched instantly from spoiled child to smiling lady. The subject changed from Flo's misbehavior to the beauty of the lighted glasshouse, as the young man joined them.

Flo yearned to do something useful with her life, something truly important. Parties? Dances? They weren't important. And yet, that's all her family wanted of her. Be a gracious daughter. Marry some socially prominent man and be a gracious wife.

Parthe and Mama—and Papa, too, Flo knew—would never let Flo even think about nursing or working among the poor. And that was the greatest war inside her.

How could Flo make her family understand? Much as she enjoyed the people she met and the things she did, she was miserable in this kind of life. And the root of her misery was her call from God. On February 7, 1837—Flo remembered the date well—God had called her to serve Him. That was five years ago, when she was seventeen, and today she wasn't a step closer to obeying Him.

As usual, the Nightingales spent Christmas at the Nicholsons'. Mama and Aunt Anne, sisters, gossiped. Cousin Marianne bustled about organizing sings and dances. Henry followed Flo around. But it was Aunt Hannah whom Flo cherished.

She thought Aunt Hannah was probably as close to an angel as mortals ever get. She knew God in person. What impressed Flo most, Aunt Hannah had found peace with God. She was content. It was Aunt Hannah and Aunt Hannah alone that Flo told about the war inside her. Here was a person to whom all unseen things seemed real and eternal things were near. She would understand.

Aunt Hannah took Flo aside one day. "My dear, I've been thinking and praying about what you've said. The first and most important way to oneness with God is to remove the sin barrier. We all start out with one, you know."

"Surely not you! You're so—so pious."

"Every human being. The payment for that sin is death. Jesus didn't have to die, but He gave His life anyway, to pay for sin so that we wouldn't have to. Do you understand that?"

"I see what you're saying."

"Accept what Jesus did, and the sin barrier will dissolve. Then as you develop oneness of mind with God, you can taste eternal contentment even here on earth."

Flo pondered that. Aunt Hannah had awakened her to the realities of the faith as no one else had ever done. And yet, she was so restless, so frustrated by forced inactivity and leisure.

The bright lights of the Chatsworth glasshouse mocked her. The bright lights of her whole lifestyle mocked her. To Flo, life was black. Black.

So you've met Flo and her family. Her family was what historians might call "typical products of the Victorian Age." That means that they thought the way everyone else thought at that time.

Except Flo. Being socially correct wasn't enough to make her happy. But the circle her family moved in gave her no chance to change.

Incidentally, the Henry that Parthe mentioned was Henry Nicholson. The Nicholsons were cousins on Flo's Mama's side. Flo didn't really have much use for Henry, but he was Marianne's favorite brother, and Flo adored Marianne. Marianne was so pretty, and so talented, and so graceful, and—Flo was just as pretty and talented and graceful, but she didn't think so. She was tall like her father—"willowy" was the term used for girls. With chestnut brown hair and a slim figure, wit and a quick mind, she far outshone her sister, Parthe.

On the outside, Flo was an attractive and happy woman. On the inside, she was miserable. But things were to get worse before they'd get better. For her family was absolutely certain Florence Nightingale must never even consider being a nurse.

2

Those Blue Books

June 1846

Papa himself designed the Nightingale traveling carriage, as he had years ago designed the remodeling of both Lea Hurst and Embley. The houses were huge and spacious. So was the carriage. Twelve people could travel in it comfortably, if you counted the seats for the servants on the roof of it.

It stood now outside the back door of Embley as servants loaded it for the annual journey north to Lea Hurst. Lord Palmerston was visiting, as he often did, and Lord Ashley was with him. Mama, Papa, and Lord Palmerston took tea in the gazebo. Flo and Lord Ashley challenged each other to a game of croquet.

At the lord's behest, Flo led off. She missed the far right wicket. And she'd been practicing, too!

With a grin Lord Ashley used her ball to advance himself to center court. "I see that Monckton Milnes is charmed with you. Most of the Palmerston match-ups don't turn out that well."

"Richard's a fine man," Flo said. "His attempts to reform the country's penal codes so that youthful prisoners aren't housed with hardened criminals, for example—I much admire that sort of thing."

Lord Ashley leaned on his mallet. "How are *you* doing, Flo? I mean, really doing, inside."

"Really? Terrible. Worse than the last time you asked. I feel so dreadfully frustrated, Ashley."

"You still like nursing, and your family still opposes."

"True. But that's only part. I know so very little about treating sick people. Often, all I can do is sit at the bedside to hold a dying person's hand. If only there were someplace where I could learn the skills I need. A hospital, perhaps. But Mama won't even consider it."

"She probably told you that hospitals are dens of sin. And she's right. I've seen them; I know."

"That doesn't help the frustration. It's not that Mama isn't charitable. She is, because performing acts of charity is part of being wealthy. And she's quite generous. Papa, too. He pays for the school near Lea Hurst. But they don't want me actually mingling with the poor who accept our charity." She frowned. "Do you see the difference?"

"Vividly. Why not read Blue Books?"

"What are Blue Books?"

"Commission reports. For example, The Poor Law commissioners put one out on medical services to the poor in East London. Then you have your hospital reports which come directly from . . ."

A grin spread across his face. "Will you continue to play or continue to stare at me?"

"I never knew Blue Books existed. How can I get them?"

"Write for them. I'll send you some of the more interesting ones from my own shelf. It's mostly dry facts and figures, but you might find a few items to chew on."

"I like nothing better than to bite down on a good solid fact! I'll be forever grateful to you, Lord Ashley!" But she wasn't *too* grateful. She tapped his ball with hers, used his to get through the next three wickets, and won the game.

Starting with Lord Ashley's, the Blue Books began arriving. They were more wonderful than Flo could have imagined. There were thousands of facts about hospitals. In a separate notebook she wrote down information from them—facts from many different sources that came together to paint new pictures of the state of hospitals and health.

She did it all in the early morning. Hours before the rest of the household awakened, Flo would rise. She would wrap a heavy shawl around her, for she hated cold. Then she would light a candle at her little table, read, and make her notes. When the breakfast bell rang she would go downstairs to begin the day that the rest of her family knew about.

The days were boring, too. After breakfast, Flo, Parthe, and Mama would all sit at the table while Papa read the *Times* newspaper aloud to them. Flo despised sitting still and being read to when she could have read it more quickly herself. Besides, the items Papa chose to read did not appeal to Flo.

Her interests and Papa's were too far apart now. Had he changed? No. Papa never changed. He hated change. Flo had changed.

Then what? Arrange flowers. Work on embroidery. Write letters. Make social arrangements. Go calling. Perhaps take a walk in the New Forest, if the weather was fine. Flo felt she was being suffocated—buried alive in a mound of useless frittering.

Flo found herself daydreaming. Dreaming isn't bad. Sometimes it's very nice. But her mind would wander when it shouldn't. She would dream about Richard Monckton Milnes, or about how she would handle a crisis, or would be called out to help in a situation because no one else knew what to do.

At one of Mama's parties Flo met a charming couple, Selena and Charles Bracebridge. Selena loved anything Greek; Papa quickly gave her a nickname—Sigma. Sigma was the Greek letter S. Sigma and Charles quickly became fast friends.

Over the winter of 1847 Charles and Sigma took Flo along with them to Europe. What a wonderful time she had! The best part was meeting in Rome a whole new circle of friends. And the brightest of them were Sidney and Liz Herbert. Sidney was handsome and wealthy and smart. Liz was beautiful. They gave most of their income each year to the needy. Flo loved them both!

Back home in England, Flo studied her Blue Books. She read the hospital reports that friends in France and Germany sent her. She filled notebooks with her charts and lists. And she read about Kaiserwerth.

Kaiserwerth was a religious medical ministry, if you had to classify it as something. They ran a hospital and a school. They had a care center for little children. And they were a religious institution, serving God. Flo's mind became filled with Kaiserwerth. If only she could study there to be a nurse! If only—

Nearly a year passed, and for the whole year Flo's misery grew. Then one day those beautiful people Sidney and Liz Herbert invited Flo—not the whole family, just Flo—to tour a home in Charmouth. She accepted with pleasure.

When Flo arrived at Charmouth she realized the invitation had been carefully worded. Reading it, Mama and Papa would not have guessed. But Charmouth was a convalescent home, a home where people who had been very ill could rest and get well. Sidney had given money to build it as a charity out of his own pocket.

Flo was not the only person invited. Others, wealthy people who gave most of their money to the needy, came also. They, like Sidney, badly wanted better hospitals.

Enthusiastically, Sidney led his group through the halls of the new building, showing them this room and that. Flo followed as if in a dream, but this was not a dream. Someone cared about the same things Flo did! She was not alone!

"Excuse me." One of Sidney's friends waved a hand. "These small private wards are going to be expensive to staff. How many people of the merchant class do you think would really make use of this facility? And for how long?"

Sidney's handsome face tightened in thought. He shook his head. "I don't know that anyone can answer that, Tom." He looked around helplessly.

Flo could. From the notebooks, from all her charts and tables, she knew. She raised her head and her voice. "The best figures on that are from France and Germany. Their merchant class is similar to ours, so I assume it's safe to compare." The numbers came to her as if she'd written them yesterday.

From the Poor Law report she could quote the number of poor requiring convalescence. From a hospital report she could quote similar figures from Germany. She remembered the tables she had made; now she could recite them.

Sidney was staring at her. He asked a question, and she knew the answer to that one, too. More questions came, and more answers. Flo suddenly got embarrassed.

As the group broke up, Flo paused beside Sidney's carriage. "I do apologize for intruding there. Very rude of me."

"Rude?" That wonderful face lit up like the Chatsworth glasshouse. "My dear Flo! You don't know what a godsend you are to us! I read the Blue Book you quoted from. Others, too. But it never occurred to me to compare facts the way you do. You made the information much more useful to us. Nor do I think anyone else is doing that sort of thing. As far as I know, you are the nation's leading authority on hospitals and nursing management."

"Come now, Sidney. You needn't try to put me at ease with flattery, much as I enjoy it. I don't—"

His face lost the smile. "I'm not flattering, Flo. You have at your fingertips a monumental body of facts and figures. And no one else in England does. I mean every word I just said." The smile came popping back as quickly as it had left. "Now permit Liz and me to treat England's greatest hospital authority to dinner before you return home."

Perhaps Flo was on the right track. Sidney's praise encouraged her and gave her hope. Perhaps God would soon use her as He promised.

Then Parthe got sick. Papa said it was nerves. Mama said it was worry because Flo was being difficult. The doctor said she needed treatments at a spa—Carlsbad, perhaps, in Germany. Flo's heart leaped. Kaiserwerth was only a few miles from Carlsbad! They could go to the spa, and she could get several weeks of hospital training. Then political trouble in Frankfurt changed Papa's mind. They would go to Malvern instead. The mineral baths were quite as good there, he said.

Malvern! That was only a short distance from home right here in England. Flo's plan to train as a nurse was dead. But Mama hadn't killed it. Papa hadn't, not deliberately. Mama and Papa never knew what Flo had in mind. No, Flo blamed God Himself. He had set the plan in her mind. Then He yanked it away, just like that. He called her to serve Him, then denied her the chance. What kind of a God was this, anyway?

He wanted something she was not yet giving Him; that much was obvious. Flo decided she was not yet good enough to be God's servant. She must improve herself. She must become more worthy. Aunt Hannah could advise her. She knew God intimately. Flo wrote to Aunt Hannah.

Aunt Hannah replied in soothing words that Flo must accept her station. Even a house party, she said, can be given to the glory of God.

Flo wrote back immediately. "How can social fluff be to the glory of God when there is so much misery in the world which we might be curing, instead of living in luxury?"

Aunt Hannah did not write back.

Flo was devastated. Aunt Hannah, it seemed, abandoned her. God had snatched Kaiserwerth out of her hand. Things could hardly get worse.

But they did.

Richard Monckton Milnes asked her to marry him. If she said yes, she could live a life of ease and fun in London. Her family wanted that; she need not struggle with them anymore.

But then she'd be just like her family, arranging flowers and frittering her life away. She'd entertain at breakfast rather than at tea, but the end was the same. If she married now, God's call was lost. And yet, serving God seemed hopeless anyway.

It tore her heart apart; but she said no.

Mama was enraged. "Ingrate!" she screamed. "He's from a fine family, an excellent family for a person of your station. We have lavished all manner of time and money on you, educating you and preparing you for marriage into a good family.

And now you say no for no good reason! It is your *duty* to us to marry him!''

"I'm sorry, Mama. I do love the man, but no. I can't.''

"You're a spoiled, ungrateful child. You just love to make our lives miserable, don't you!''

"You're miserable? Mama, you don't understand the half of my misery. I—''

"I understand this. You will not have your selfish way. Your foolish fancies about hospitals and nursing are done, Florence Nightingale! That nonsense is finished!''

Now you realize that Mama was wrong. Years later, when the world declared Florence a heroine, her family still did not appreciate how great were her gifts to mankind. They never did understand her. They never could see things the way she did.

And neither could dear old Aunt Hannah. Flo blamed herself for not agreeing with dear, pious Aunt Hannah. But the woman who knew God so intimately did not understand Flo. Aunt Hannah's mind simply could not grasp what Flo was trying to say. She could not see service to God the same way Flo saw it.

It was beginning to look as if no one did. Every Victorian girl was supposed to yearn to marry a man like Richard; Flo had just turned him down. No proper girl would dream of being a nurse; Flo dreamed of it constantly. A good girl obeyed her parents and behaved as they thought best. What was wrong with her?!

In modern words, poor, confused Flo was heading straight into a nervous breakdown. It was not Mama or Papa or Parthe who saved her. They couldn't see the promise in her. Sigma and Charles saw. So did Sidney and Liz. They rescued her. But even they could not see the future, when their lives would become twined and tangled with a legend.

3

From Egypt to Gentlewomen in Distressed Circumstances

March 1850

"As Rome has done me some good, the family is going to send me farther afield in hopes that that will do me even better."

Flo had written those words to her favorite cousin, Hilary Bonham Carter. How true they were. She sat today outside her little cabin at Wadi Halfa in Egypt and waited. Here came Charles and Sigma. Time to go. She stood up and walked down to the shore.

Felucca. That was the name of this little Egyptian sailboat. When the wind was right, or they were struggling upstream, the boatmen hoisted an ungainly sail. Today, though, they were cruising downstream. Flo and the Bracebridges boarded. The boatmen pushed out into the current with poles and let the mighty Nile do the work.

The mudbrick city of Wadi Halfa disappeared behind them. Flo wished her troubles could dissolve in the distance that easily.

Constant sunshine poured out of the cloudless sky. That should warm the cockles of a cold-hating girl's heart; she felt indifferent to it. They explored the ruins of Karnak; the Bracebridges clambered about and oohed and aahed. Flo sat on the steps of the great temple and daydreamed.

It wasn't all dreaming. God seemed to speak to her there, a gentle reminder of His presence and His desire for her service. *Yes, God, but then why all the barriers? Why the problems?* And would she give five minutes of every hour to thought of Him?

Was this really God speaking to her? She was certain. Yes. He was God now just as He was back when these ruins were built to other gods. When Abraham tended sheep and Adam tilled the garden. Why shouldn't He be close beside her now?

They left Egypt and sailed to Greece. The Bracebridges enjoyed dazzling sunsets, emerald islands, the peaceful little coastal villages. Flo daydreamed.

Flo picked up some pets along the way. Two tortoises named Mr. and Mrs. Hill didn't provide much affection, but she liked them. And she caught a cicada. Cicadas symbolize wisdom. She named it Plato and waited for it to chirp something wise. It offered her no more comfort than did the tortoises or her family.

In Athens, the Bracebridges eagerly toured the Parthenon. They asked questions of their guide, and Sigma practiced her Greek. Flo wandered aimlessly outside, daydreaming.

Some things never change. Here were some small boys doing what small boys must have been doing for the last two thousand years: throwing stones at the Parthenon. She stepped in behind them, curious. What was their target?

A tiny owl huddled in a niche in the building stones as rocks pelted all around it. Every feather stuck straight out.

"Stop!" Papa had taught Flo classical Greek, not the modern language. But it apparently worked well enough. The boys wheeled around to stare at her.

"For whom is this city named?" Flo asked in Greek.

"Athena," one of the bolder boys replied.

"And what creature is Athena's symbol?"

"The owl," he muttered.

"Shame! Trying to hurt a little owl in Athena's city in her temple! Begone!"

Apparently an Englishwoman spouting history and defending a dumb old owl was too much to take. They scampered off.

Rescuing an owl that does not want to be rescued is very, very hard. Flo could just barely crawl up high enough to reach it. The owl considered her as much an enemy as the boys and pecked her savagely. She wrapped it in her handkerchief to save her skin.

She carried the owl in her pocket until she could buy a small cage for it. But once it got used to her, it seemed to prefer traveling in her pocket. She carried it everywhere that way. She named it Athena.

The Bracebridges decided to return to England overland through Europe. So, Flo daydreamed her way across Europe with an owl in her pocket. She forgot, however, that natural laws govern predators and prey, owls and insects. In Prague, Athena ate Plato.

Sigma, bless her, had arranged this overland route for a special reason—to let Flo visit Kaiserwerth! From Germany home, Flo was a new and happy woman.

Two weeks later, though, she had plunged again to the depths. When Mama found out about Kaiserwerth she raged. Parthe dissolved in hysterics. Papa hid.

Mama laid down the law. Flo had spent six months playing on two continents and disgracing the family in Germany, Mama said. And all the while her poor sister pined at home. For the next six months, Flo must devote herself to Parthe. Flo would do whatever Parthe wanted and be her companion.

"Mama, Parthe is thirty-one years old! I'm insane to accept a yoke of slavery. This whole household is insane!" But Flo lost, of course. Mama always won.

What a horrible, miserable six months! Parthe pouted. She demanded. She whined and complained. And Flo had to pamper her. The moment her torment ended, Flo fled to visit Sidney and Liz Herbert. A rest at their house healed her shattered nerves. It didn't hurt that the Herbert home was perhaps the loveliest estate in all England.

And the truth slowly, oh, so slowly, began to dawn. Flo's grandfather Smith loved a party as much as Mama. But he gave away money generously and worked hard for reforms. Richard Monckton Milnes gave freely and fought for prison reform. Already Lord Ashley had played a major role in getting the corn laws repealed. Now he was tackling factory workers' conditions.

The Herberts? They spent most of their income on hospital reform. Sidney served as war secretary and secretary to the Admiralty, among other positions. The Bracebridges cared about people. These people all had as much money as Papa— even more. They all entertained as beautifully as Mama did. But their lives counted for something! They helped people!

Mama shrieked and raged. Parthe threw hysterics. But that didn't make their opinion right. The utter foolishness of that six-month enslavement finally brought Flo to her senses. She would waste no more of her life. At last she saw that she must break free, for her family would never let her go themselves. In June of 1851, Flo announced that she would train for nursing at Kaiserwerth.

Although Flo took charge, two years later she still wasn't serving God. Not yet, but service, at long last, was in sight.

She had been to Kaiserwerth. She had learned important lessons in hospital management and administration. But she learned no nursing at all. Fine an institution as it was, the skills of its nurses were no higher than what Flo knew already. It had not been at all what she expected.

As soon as she got home Mama pulled her back into the social whirl. It was the same old life. It was as if Mama were trying to erase some horrid black mark from the family slate. But then Liz Herbert heard about the Institution for the Care of Sick Gentlewomen in Distressed Circumstances. They needed a director. Liz knew just who it should be. In a matter of weeks, Flo applied, was interviewed, and got the job.

On August 12, 1853, Flo entered the Institution's doors at 1 Harley Street and found the first real happiness of her life.

The commissioners were not convinced that Liz Herbert was right. A lady this young and fragile looking was not the director they had in mind. Perhaps if the young lady had an older woman of some sort on the premises—? Flo invited Aunt Mai to help out, and they went to work.

The Institution had gone broke once. If it was to avoid going broke again, Flo must watch every penny. One thing that made Mama's parties such successes was that Mama personally attended every detail. From her Flo had learned well to attend to details.

Mama had put her in charge of the pantry those years ago. That training came in very handy now. At Embley she had counted jam pots. Here she put the hospital kitchen to work making jam. They saved a shilling a pot over grocers' prices.

The grocer's boy came around several times daily, delivering foods at by-the-ounce prices. Flo contracted with wholesalers for bulk quantities at huge savings.

The doctors prescribed medicines. The druggists' assistants then came around from the apothecary shops to dispense the medicines. Flo convinced the doctors to both prescribe and dispense, bought the medicine in quantity, and saved five hundred pounds right there.

The coalman stuck his grimy head in the office door. "Coal's delivered, Mum. 'Tis customary to be paid on delivery, ye know."

"Thank you. I shall inspect." Flo hiked her skirts and picked up a rake on her way downstairs.

He watched her from the coal window. "Mum? Ye surely don't care to spoil y'r clothes down there. All coal looks 'bout the same, ye know. Black as coal."

"But it doesn't all burn the same."

She raked through the pile. It was as she suspected. She left the rake at the bottom of the stairs.

She brushed her hands off on the way to her desk. She'd wash up later. "That's not a full load, as we both well know; too much coal dust for the amount of coal. Add a couple hundredweight, and we'll call it even."

"I've no more coal in me rig."

"Then we'll adjust the bill accordingly." She picked up her pen and the checks.

"Uh, Mum? Ye plan to rake through every load delivered?"

"Every load."

"I'll tell me superiors so."

Flo smiled and wrote out the check.

This pinching every penny was very new to Flo. In her family no expense was ever spared. Now suddenly not a shilling dared be wasted. She loved the challenge, frustrating as it was at times.

In October Aunt Mai stepped inside the office. "Liz Herbert and Lady Canning to see you."

"Ask Molly to serve tea." Flo put her work aside instantly. It was always a treat to see Liz.

She met them in the hall as Liz was lifting off her little poke bonnet. A hug and a handshake and they greeted all around.

Liz was so beautiful when she smiled. "Lady Canning and I were talking about those pages and pages of instructions you sent while the building was being remodeled. Windlasses? Bells and whistles? We stopped by to see if any of it's working."

"It all is. Come see!" Flo led the way down the hall. She stopped near the nurses' station. "Bells and whistles." She pointed to a panel high in the wall.

Liz frowned. "Little valves? Are those the valves?"

"Those are the valves. When the patient rings the bell by her bed, the valve toots and flies open out here. The nurse looks up and sees instantly which bed has rung. Saves all manner of time and steps."

"I never heard of such a thing." Lady Canning stared.

"There was no such thing. I designed it to meet a need." Flo led on down the hall to the end. "You ask about windlasses. They were installed in this dumbwaiter."

"What's below. The kitchen?" Liz opened the little door in the wall and peered down the dark hollow shaft.

"Yes. The kitchen crew puts the hot meals for this floor in the dumbwaiter. With the windlass the nurse cranks it up to her floor here, removes the food—"

"Sends the dumbwaiter down for the next load and delivers the food still hot to her patients! How clever!"

Flo nodded. "Shall we go to the parlor for tea?"

"Let's!" Liz even led the way. She did enjoy her tea. "Flo, you look so good! Things must be going very smoothly here."

"Smoothly? Hardly! The committees haven't a penny left. We need saucepans and kitchen supplies. We're making bedclothes out of old curtains. I sent some of the worst linen down to Embley to be washed and patched."

Liz cleared her throat. "I apologize for sounding catty, Flo, and I don't mean it so. But I'm surprised your mother would consent to that. You and nursing—"

"Mama has her own ideas about what is proper. But she also knows her duty as a lady. She's always been generous with charity. I tell her the need, and she provides—and more! Every week she sends fruit and vegetables, flowers and game up from Embley, quite on her own."

"So you and your family are reconciled?"

"It's more an uneasy truce. Papa keeps suggesting I should limit my nursing to babies—you know, something proper. Parthe came to visit and collapsed in hysterics at the door. Mama still won't give her blessing, but she doesn't rage."

Flo entered her little sitting room. The maid had her blue teacups all set up and waiting. "Liz, in the last three months I've learned how to supply a hospital without spending any money. It's not a lesson I enjoy, and I hope I never have to use that lesson again. Now let's talk of more pleasant things. Tell me how Sidney is doing."

Because you're a clever reader, you see by now what Flo's family's problem was. To her Mama, social position was everything. And Mama was terrified that Flo might damage it somehow—cast a shadow on the Nightingale name with her dabbling in such an immoral pastime as nursing.

And Parthe? Her case was even sadder. The plain sister was not as attractive or witty. Her prettier sister had all the lovers and the glittering friends. Any glory Parthe enjoyed was glory reflected from Flo. If Flo were to make a fool of herself or bring shame on her own head, Parthe's glory fled as well. And Parthe got all her ideas about what is proper from her mother.

But then, you figured that out; and you've good company. Dr. Clark, the queen's personal physician, was the Nightingales' doctor also. He said exactly the same thing. He suggested years before Flo left home that Parthe be sent somewhere apart, to rest. "Nonsense!" said Mama. "It's only nerves." And she planned more parties. In the end, Parthe survived her emotional problem and she survived Mama's cure as well.

And what about our Flo? Flo had found her niche. She was answering her call. After thirty-three years, all was finally right in her world.

4

Cholera

Summer 1854

The sorriest, oldest, raggedest horses in the world drew the hansom cabs of London. Flo was sure of it. From her office window she watched a cab pull up to the hospital door. It's motheaten gray nag took not one step more than it had to. When it clip-clopped to a lazy stop, it was absolutely stopped, its nose nearer to the street cobbles than to its own ears. The horse looked more in need of hospitalization than did the young woman climbing out of the cab.

The girl turned instantly and reached inside the cab to help someone else. The cabbie hopped down to give a hand. The patient-to-be was a girl even younger than this first woman. So weak she could not stand, she simply draped like a wet rag between the two as they hoisted her up the steps.

Flo ran to the hall and yanked the front door open. She called to the clerk, "A wheeled stretcher; instantly!"

As they came staggering through the door, the smell pushed Flo back a step. The poor girl had no control at all of anything. She flopped, a heavy heap, into the wooden chair by the door.

Her companion was wide-eyed. "It happened so fast, Mum. She was fine as rain one minute, and the next—she didn't even have time to make it to the loo. Moaning and howling, in wretched pain she was. Still is. Something she ate, aye, Mum?"

Flo glanced at the cabbie.

"I seen it many a time." He wagged his head. "Cholera. We had it in forty-five and in forty-nine. Now here 'tis again. Seems like working girls get it the worst, too."

Flo looked at the girl's upset companion. "There's no need you stay. She'll be in the back without visitors, and she'll be here a while. Days. Perhaps the cabbie will see you home now."

"Please, Mum, can I help with her? She's got no kin."

"The pauper hospitals expect friends and relatives to come in and nurse the sick, but we do not. We've a fine professional staff. And Dr. Bowman is here today. The best care anywhere." Flo smiled. "Believe me. You're safer home."

Here came the wheeled stretcher rattling down the hall. Flo must see about oiling the squeak in it. The orderly picked up the girl in one big armful and dumped her on the cart. Away it went back up the hall. Fast. Effective. But it surely didn't look very professional to a London cabbie or to a young lady concerned about her friend's sickness. Flo would speak to the orderly later. It was not a matter for the moment.

"Give our admitting clerk here the particulars about your friend, please—name, age, and such. Thank you." Flo turned toward the hall and turned again, pausing. "Where is she from?"

"Soho, Mum. Molly. Her name is Molly."

"Thank you." Not the best part of town. Not even a good part of town. When disease cut loose in a district like Soho, it almost always spread very quickly. Flo ran down the hall.

The orderly and a young nurse were stripping the girl's soiled clothes away. Flo helped sponge clean the pale body. Molly began moaning. The room filled with a heavy, repulsive stench.

Like a whirlwind, in blew Dr. Bowman, a large man who filled rooms simply by entering them. He looked grimly at the girl and wagged his head. "Flo, I suggest you send Marcia out to the chemists* for as much morphine as she can find. By tomorrow, I wager, there will be none left in the city. Get it while we can."

Flo pointed to the orderly. "See to it, please!"

He nodded and left hastily.

The doctor gave Molly a dose of morphine—a large dose, Flo thought. By degrees the moaning abated to a whimper.

In the next half hour, as Flo watched shocked, Molly shriveled up before her eyes. Her skin turned

*The person who in America is called a pharmacist or druggist.

dry and began to take on a blue cast. Her round cheeks shrank and grew haggard. Her eyes —very pretty eyes—sank back in her head. And how cold and clammy her hands were, as if she had been out in winter rain.

Cholera. Everyone had heard of it. Anyone could tell you it was a deadly disease that caused vomiting and diarrhea. From her work with the Blue Books Flo knew that of every ten people who got it, five would die.

"Here's another, Mum!" called the orderly from the hallway. "Came from clear over on Broad Street. Her friends heard we're the best hospital in town."

Before nightfall another cholera case was brought in, this one from St. Giles. By morning the hospital housed patients from Shoreditch and Mayfair, too, and neither Flo nor Dr. Bowman had slept at all.

At mid-morning, after admitting two more cholera cases, Flo and the doctor paused for tea and biscuits in Flo's study.

She sank into her wingback chair, and closed her burning eyes. "I do hope this is the end now."

"You hope in vain. It's not even the beginning."

Her eyes popped open. "You don't know that, Doctor."

"I do know it, Flo. Nine, ten years ago, a particularly bad epidemic broke out; not just here, either. Even over in America, people migrating in wagons to their west coast seeded it among the natives. Thousands of red Indians died, and thousands of Americans."

"Yes, but this is hardly America."

"Oh, it was here, much worse than you realize. You see, in England it strikes the lower classes hardest. When a lord or lady dies, that's news. But you don't hear about it when the poor drop over by the score. Five years ago a Doctor Snow found the cause. Dirty drinking water."

"Yes, but . . ."

"He demonstrated it. Proved it. Urged the city government to take action and provide clean drinking water. Not a thing—not a solitary thing—was done. Now here we are again." The doctor sighed and closed his eyes. "Ought to get the Lord Mayor in here to carry the corpses out. Maybe then he'd see the light."

"This Doctor Snow proved it?"

"Convincingly."

Flo opened her mouth to ask the next question; obviously, Dr. Bowman had made quite a study of cholera, to know so much about its influence in foreign countries; but the orderly stuck his head in the door.

"Doctor! You're needed straightway."

And they were off again.

Day after day, week after week, the cholera patients came. Half were carried out in boxes, their agony cut short by death. Horrible as it was, the dying was only part. There was also the mess, the sheer mess, that this ugly epidemic caused. What do you do with all the dirty clothes, the filthy bedding, the soiled cleaning rags? Where do you dump the buckets?

Flo heard, in the midst of the horror, that England and Turkey had decided to make war with Russia. *Hostilities*, it was politely called. Poor Sidney Herbert! He had been appointed the Secretary at War, a great honor. But now he who loved mankind and hated war was suddenly in the middle of it. Then the war in those distant lands was eclipsed by the war against death right here in the Institution for Sick Gentlewomen in Distressed Circumstances.

Two of the nurses quit in fear. Their cowardice outraged Flo—until she saw Middlesex. In August, Middlesex Hospital desperately needed someone to superintend the cholera nursing there. Flo volunteered.

Middlesex Hospital had lost far more than two nurses. Several had already died; others had run away in fear. Even some of the doctors were fleeing into the country. Although cholera struck anywhere it chose, it seemed most often to choose the cities, with their crowded districts and faulty water supply.

September came, and the first of the autumn rains. A whole day passed with no new admissions. New cases slowed to a trickle. They ceased, or nearly so.

It was over.

Intensely, completely weary, Flo returned to Harley Street.

Toward the last of September, Sidney Herbert stopped by for a visit. He was as handsome and stately as ever, but worry lines had begun to write stories of overwork and sadness around the creases of his eyes. The maid led him into Flo's little parlor and hurried off to fetch tea.

He kissed Flo's hand, elegant as always, and flopped into the morocco leather chair. "You lost weight this summer, Flo. You can ill afford it, you know. You were already slim as a fence rail. Eat more. Get more rest."

"Ah, see the pot calling the kettle black. You've had a rough time lately, too.

"War. Rumors of wars." He sighed.

"My dear Mr. Herbert, you are the nation's Secretary of War. The powers that be declare them, then dump them in your lap. 'Tis their role and yours."

"And we all play our roles. Yes. You're doing fine in yours. Liz receives splendid reports about the success and efficiency of this hospital."

"Our day-to-day costs are half what they were before I took over, and we handle more patients. It's all a matter of finding the right suppliers. And dispensing drugs efficiently."

"They also save the cost of your salary. You're the only one here who doesn't get paid."

She shrugged. "My father gives me five hundred pounds a year. I always overspend it." She sat forward as tea arrived.

"I know better than most how long you worked and yearned for this. I'm very happy for you."

"Thank you. But do you know? The place is running smoothly. It doesn't need me anymore. I'm ready to move on."

"On to where?"

"I've been talking to Dr. Bowman. He serves here only part time. His senior position is at Kings College Hospital."

"I hear it's going to be completely rebuilt."

"Yes. I've been urging him to have a school of nursing built right into it. A facility to train superior nurses."

Sidney exploded in laughter. "And appoint you superintendent of the school."

"But of course." She poured tea and handed him his cup. "A doctor I met several years ago in Paris wrote recently. He asked me to recommend some reliable nurses to serve in hospitals in the colonies. Reliable? Sidney, I couldn't. I have no fish of that kind."

"Ah, but if I can push the reforms through that I have in mind, nursing conditions will be much improved."

"What good are better conditions without better nurses? I want to start a system of schools to produce good nurses. Women of honor who can command the same respect doctors do."

"Impossible. It can't be done. Nursing will always be looked down on." He smiled suddenly. "But bless you for wanting to."

She sat back. "And now, dear friend, how goes the war?"

"The cholera has been striking world-wide. It's a worse enemy than the Russians. Our troops fighting in Turkey and the Crimea are staging at Varna. Apparently cholera is epidemic at Varna. But I'm told conditions are improving and things are looking up."

"I hear doubt in your voice."

"I never trust the words of men who are paid to provide rosy reports. However, I have no reason not to believe them. So, in answer to your question, the war is apparently going as well as any war can be expected to." He lifted his cup. "To your nurses and your nursing, Flo. May they prosper even as the war in the Crimea dries up."

"Amen." And she tapped his cup with hers.

Friday the thirteenth of October, Dr. Bowman came whirling into the hospital as usual, all bustle and business.

He whipped a *London Times* paper out from under his arm and stuck it in front of Flo's nose. "Read this." A very long article was circled in red ink.

"William Howard Russell. Who's he?"

"Reporter for the *Times*. Went out with the British troops to the war in the Crimea, and he's been filing shocking reports."

"Sidney says his people have been telling him all is going well."

"Russell says differently. The troops landed in the Crimea with no medical supplies at all—no room for them on the ship, so they were left behind. Cholera filled the hospitals before the first war casualty ever arrived. Cases left untreated. No stores, no bandages, no medicines, no supplies of any kind. Hospital ships are nothing more than old freighters. He says here that one ship, for example, was outfitted to carry two hundred and fifty casualties. She took fifteen hundred men, her first trip."

"I can't believe this."

"The rest of England believes him. And it's all coming down on the head of your friend Sidney Herbert."

She stared blankly at the newspaper. "Thank you, doctor. If you'll excuse me—" She brushed past him, that terrible news report leaping and clawing at her eyes. Poor Sidney! Poor, poor Sidney.

She sat down in her little parlor and called for tea. She must think. By the time tea arrived she knew what she must do. As she sipped the first cup of scalding brew she knew how she would do it. She would ask Sidney to send her to the Crimea with a picked crew of nurses. With the second cup she decided how she would go about choosing them.

Yes! That was it. Exactly. She would write Sidney instantly. The business was settled already in her mind. In a matter of weeks she would be on a boat headed for the Crimea.

Is it too bold to say that Flo was at last fulfilling that call from God she heard so many years before? For even as she was writing to her friend Sidney, he was writing to her, asking her to superintend a crew of trained nurses in the Crimea. Their letters crossed; and both letters (as was the custom between Flo and Sidney) ended with "God bless you."

She had a terrible time finding good nurses! But find them she did, and they sailed a few weeks later. Crowds in England saw them off.

Crowds in France greeted them as they passed through, and cheered them on their way.

Blue Books, wrangling with committees, pinching every penny, making do with nothing, managing a hospital, feeding patients, dealing with a massive cholera epidemic—it was all training for this next task. Handling those problems had prepared her, and good thing, too, for she was sailing straight into disaster.

You might say it was all a dress rehearsal for one of the greatest tragic dramas the world has ever seen. Florence Nightingale would take center stage in that drama. And she herself would change the face of war forever.

5

Scutari Nightmare

November 1854

   These were called caiques—open rowboats, painted with wild designs in vivid, breezy colors. They
practically glowed, bright under the overcast sky.
Riding in peaceful, quiet gondolas in Venice had
not prepared Flo for this. She watched from the
rail of the ship as her nurses one by one clambered
over the side into the little boats. Turkish boatmen rowed them from the steamship offshore to
land, for there was no dock big enough for a ship
this size on the Scutari side of the Bosporus.
   Scutari. Flo studied the shore opposite the strait
from the city of Constantinople, for this was where
she and her nurses would serve. The hospital—
their hospital—stood like a huge gray box on the
hilltop crest above the water. A cluster of tents
and sheds huddled at the foot of the steep slope.
Flo turned to Charles Bracebridge leaning on the
rail beside her. "The village of Scutari doesn't have

many buildings, it appears. Except that great square barracks, of course."

"Scutari's where Constantinople put her cemetery, Flo. Then the Turks built their army barracks—the block structure you see—and the hospital beside it, that building just beyond. Turks aren't using it, so we are. The tents and all are local people who have moved in, so to speak, to trade with the British soldiers."

"I'm sure. Mr. Russell's articles said the hospital is full, and the barracks is now a hospital also."

"Right. We're to serve in the Barracks Hospital."

Sigma nudged up to the rail between Flo and Charles. "Is that nice Lord Napier we met the person in charge?"

Charles grimaced. "Wish he were. Lord Stratford is. A Dr. Menzies is in charge of the hospitals, and a Major Sillery is the military commandant. However, we won't be concerned with any of them. The nurses will work for the doctors themselves."

It sounded like a simple chain of command. Flo knew enough about British chains of command, though, to know that nothing is simple.

Now it was her turn to climb down from the ship into a caique, and she dreaded it. A seaman she was not. The ferry from England to France? Not bad. And short. She genuinely enjoyed the carriage journey across France. But the sea voyage from France to Malta to here? Disastrous! Ill, too weak to lift her head, she had traveled the whole way lying flat on her back, feeling wretched. Praise God it was over!

Now if she could just make it these last few lurching, bobbing yards to shore—she was over the side, hanging between sky and sloshing water. She was in this hideously unstable little boat. Now her Turkish boatman was rowing merrily, his grin a dental catastrophe of crooked brown teeth. Finally his boat nudged a rickety pier, and now willing hands were helping her stand, lifting her out. She might as well walk on the water, so unstable was this pier.

At last, solid land! Flo climbed the shore a short way and turned to look, to really look for the first time, at the new world around her. Constantinople stretched up and down the far shore. Round domes of mosques and sharp spires of minarets gave it an other-worldly appearance. Even from here she could see the tiny splashes of color that were the tent roofs of bazaars and little hidden markets along the city's crooked streets. To the north of town an ancient fortress perched on the edge between land and water and scowled at the gray sky. The sky scowled back just as darkly.

Sigma and Charles were safely ashore now. Her nurses waited impatiently. Time to walk up the steep road to the Barracks Hospital. Why did Flo feel such a grim sense of foreboding?

Surely workmen of some sort would repair this road to the barracks shortly. It was a track—less than a track—with ruts and rocks and washed-out stretches.

Here came two local men, barefoot fellows with teeth as brown as the boatman's.

Flo hailed the nearer. "Excuse me. Is this the only road to the Barracks Hospital?"

"There." He pointed to the great gray block of a building.

"Yes. But if I wanted to go there another way— is there another road?"

He thought a moment. "This way. Up this way. Walk. Ride mule. Want mules? I get you mules. Ten *piastres*, you ride in style, eh?"

"No, thank you. How do the wounded men get there? The sick?"

"Walk. Ride mule. Maybe we carry some, stretchers, eh? You tired? We carry you. Ten *piastres*."

She forced a smile. "I'll walk, but thank you very much." She started forward again. "Charles, how the soldiers must suffer! Hurting already, and then they have to jiggle up this road in those clumsy hospital wagons."

"I don't think you realize what that fellow was saying. There are no carts, Flo. You can't get a wagon up this track. I'll bet every wounded man, every ounce of supplies, is carried up by hand."

Sigma snorted. "Ridiculous, Charles!"

Ridiculous, indeed; but true. Every single ounce, by hand. She turned and watched downhill as Turkish porters picked up the first of their parcels and started this way.

And now she was walking through the yawning gray gate, and a chill ran down her back. She could smell it out here, before ever she stepped inside. Sewage. Cholera.

Cold, blank walls wrapped themselves around them; high ceilings blotted out light and air. The hospital purveyor himself showed them to their rooms. "A bit short-handed, we are," explained Mr. Ward.

Their rooms were empty. Bare floors, bare walls, bare ceiling. Flo stood in the middle of the biggest, which was not big. "Three rooms for nearly forty people, Mr. Ward?"

"You've also a fourth room upstairs. And that fine closet."

"Closet. Yes. What are these low shelves along the walls?"

"Those are instead of beds. Turkish divans we call them. You put your bedding on them."

"I see no bedding."

"Some items are in short supply at the moment."

"We'll need tables. Chairs. Lamps or candles."

"None available, ma'am, but we're working on it."

"Lavatory supplies; washbasins. Eating utensils."

"Sorry, ma'am." He shrugged. He didn't look very sorry.

Flo stared at him. "Why do I feel so unwelcome?"

Unwelcome. They retired that night—all thirty-eight of them in four rooms plus a closet—to sleep on the hard wood Turkish divans, without lights or bedding.

Next morning Flo found the flaw in the chain of command. She and her nurses were at the doctors' disposal, to do what the doctors ordered. But the doctors refused to use her. Did they feel she was a spy for the War Department? A nuisance? Both, perhaps. Whatever, Flo's nurses sat idle in their empty rooms. She eventually found them some linen to roll into bandages.

More wounded soldiers came, boatloads of them, but the nurses sat uncalled and unused. Nurses would stand by the window watching the sorry parade of suffering men climb the hill, and cry.

Flo went exploring. She ought learn the layout of the building. But more, she must know which was true—Russell's newspaper articles or the rosy reports sent to Sidney. Russell won the grisly contest hands down.

There were not enough orderlies. There were not enough basic supplies. Patients arrived cold, wet, and filthy and remained cold, wet, and filthy. There were no operating tables. Amputations were performed right in the wards as hundreds of men watched—or tried not to.

All around her things cried out to be done. All around her needs cried out to be met. Soldiers were suffering. Dying. She could do nothing and provide nothing until the doctors asked. The waste —the sadness—appalled her. Feeling very tired and useless, she plodded up the steps toward the nurses' quarters.

On the way, she nearly bumped into a brisk, impatient looking man in a civilian suit and tie.

He stood above her on the stairs. "One of the Nightingale party, I presume."

"The Nightingale herself. Have we met, sir?"

"MacDonald, London *Times*. So have you come to sip tea, right all the wrongs, and spy for Sidney

Herbert?" Was the man really hostile, or was he testing her?

She matched his voice strength for strength, pitch for pitch, in no mood to be humble. "Apparently the doctors think so. What do you think, Mr. MacDonald?"

He studied her a moment with a bemused half smile. "I was expecting a society lady, all fluff and feathers. I don't think that's what I'm seeing. What do I think? There are so many things to be done and needs to be met, and my hands are tied because of petty men. That's what I think."

"MacDonald. I've heard your name. You were sent to administer the *Times* fund—the money for the troops that the *Times* collected. There's a small lounge near the front entrance. Join me there."

He looked a bit confused as he followed her. Two wooden chairs waited near the window. She sat down. He hesitated, then plopped down in the other.

She folded her hands. "Were this simply a matter of whom to invite to a summer party I'd go upstairs and fret in private. But men's lives are slipping through our fingers every hour that we wait. You see the urgency. I see the urgency. It's up to us to act, for these pompous fools will not."

"But how?"

"I'm sure God didn't send us here to observe while His souls die. But I will not use my nurses except by request of the doctors. If I barge in over their heads now, they'll never trust me."

"Why do you care if they trust you?"

"I'm not here simply to help out in the present crisis. I want to prove that female nurses are both useful and appropriate in military hospitals. I'm out to prove the worth of nurses."

"You'll go home without ever doing anything; they won't use you. They've united. They erected a wall, and none dares break it down." He started to rise.

She raised a hand. "There's still your problem —putting your *Times* fund to good use. Let's work on that. How much is it?"

"Thirty thousand pounds."

She found herself gaping and quickly rearranged her face. "Then the sky is indeed the limit. And no time to waste. Think!"

As he studied her, his own face changed, softening from angry to thoughtful. Here was a challenge; and apparently, like Flo, he responded well to challenges. "Each soldier was issued knives, forks, tin plates and such. Our patients were told by their officers to leave theirs behind when they came here. They did. Now the hospital says it can't supply such things because they are issued in the field. So the men have no way to cut their food, much less handle it. They do their best to eat without forks and plates. And the British are supposed to be civilized. Preposterous!"

"Yes. Eating utensils aren't a medical matter, and the doctors concern themselves only with medical matters."

A smile spread across his face. "The hospital says they're not hospital issue, and the doctors say they're not medical issue. Therefore it doesn't matter where they come from! If we choose to provide them, no regulation either allows or prevents us."

"One of the world's greatest trade cities lies across the strait. You can buy whatever you want in Constantinople. Knives, forks, spoons, plates—for every patient."

"And warm shirts. These men are still in summer uniform."

"That's right!" Flo was beginning to feel excitement for the first time since coming. "Neither the hospital nor the army will supply them. The army claims that the latest shipment of wool shirts hasn't been checked by the inspectors yet. So they sit in some warehouse. And they aren't a medical supply."

"If the army by some miracle decides to order those things, they can simply pay the *Times* fund back." He leaped to his feet. "I'll try to find a caique right now, this morning."

"Wait." She raised a hand. He sat down again. "In my tours of the hospital, Mr. MacDonald, I noticed other things that are neither medical nor army issue. Screens, to be set up around the men undergoing amputations. The men about to lose limbs should not have to watch while their comrades are hacked apart."

"Blankets. The poor wretches have only the single filthy blanket they arrived with. I asked about blankets. Mr. Ward assures me there are plenty. Somewhere. However, he can't issue any without proper authorization."

"And pillows. The men lie with their heads resting on their boots."

The man was actually smiling. Anticipation does wonders for the soul. "Perhaps also we can hire competent washerwomen. The men hide their clothes when the laundry cart comes by."

"Why?"

"The laundryman, a Greek, simply rinses them out in cold water. Doesn't get them clean, doesn't drown a single louse. The men prefer to keep their own lice, they say."

"Let's do better than just washerwomen. While you're in town, price boilers. If we could wash and boil right here, it would save much effort and time. But will you first, please, get scrub brushes and burlap? We will clean the filthy floors, including the floors in our own rooms."

"They're that bad, eh?"

"Worse. When my Sellonite nursing sisters walked into their room upstairs they found a dead man in it, stiff as a railroad tie. The room has been cleaned up, but some of his hair is still floating around on the floor."

A young man in a blood-smeared butcher's apron poked his head in the door. "There you are, mum. Dr. McGrigor wishes that ye bring y'rself and two of y'r ladies to his ward immediately."

Flo smiled at Mr. MacDonald. "I detect a crack in the wall. God bless your prowling in the bazaars of Constantinople."

He rose as she did. "And God bless your nursing, Florence Nightingale."

It was hard—very hard—to watch men suffer while all those nurses sat waiting. But it paid off. The doctors saw that Flo and her women could be trusted. When given an order they would do it. When a rule was made they would follow it. Starting with Dr. McGrigor, the doctors' resistance melted.

It had to. Conditions had been horrible before. They became a hundred times more horrible as November slipped into December. With gun and mortar, the Russians wounded many. That is war.

The wounded were brought to Scutari.

The British army at Sebastopol ran short of supplies and cooking fuel. Hungry soldiers ripped up every bush in the region, trying to stay warm and well and perhaps fix a bite to eat.

And the growing numbers of ill were brought to Scutari.

Rain and high winds ripped away tent covers and roofs, including the covers on the field hospitals there. Cold and wet, men got sick, and the wounded got sicker. Before long the sick outnumbered the well.

And they were all brought to Scutari.

The wards filled. The halls filled. There was not so much as floor space left.

And still more were brought to Scutari.

One clear head—one calm person—emerged from this insane chaos. Flo. She and Mr. MacDonald made a splendid team. She walked the wards identifying needs, and he prowled the bazaars, buying supplies to fill them.

When the wards got too crowded, Flo out of her own pocket had a useless, damaged wing repaired and cleaned up to receive another thousand patients. With her own money she purchased operating tables. Twice, for the first were burned when fuel ran short.

Flo searched the hospital, finding supplies when the army claimed no supplies existed. The doctors, the kitchen crew—even Mr. Ward himself —knew where to go when they needed something: "Ask Miss Nightingale." The hospital would have collapsed without her.

Two years later, safely home in England, Flo would say, "I have seen hell, and I cannot forget." Those first few months at Scutari burned themselves into her. They seared her memories forever. They planted themselves in her heart and became the goad that would drive her the rest of her life.

6

Nurse in Charge

Midwinter 1854-55

"Miss Nightingale, this cannot go on! It simply is not done. One does not correct all wrongs, real or fancied, by writing a check!" Pacing back and forth, Dr. Menzies waved his arms around.

Flo sat qietly and kept her hands folded in her lap. He paused in the middle of the little room. "Now I must insist you stop this meddling. I appreciate that you, as a lady of the upper class, expect to have your way when you want it, but there are regulations in the army, and you are flouting them." He paused to catch his breath.

She took advantage of the pause. "Doctor, I remind you I have never broken a rule since coming here. My nurses and I observe every regulation —nothing for a patient except by the doctor's orders. Every one. And many's the time my nurses or I have disagreed in our hearts with doctors' orders. We have bent our will to the doctors', always."

"Those are not the regulations to which I refer."

"In reference to the matter of the new boilers: Is there a regulation ordering you to install boilers?"

"No, which is the point!"

"Doctor, with all respect, the point is: There is no regulation preventing the installation of boilers, either; we checked. Since we got them, we are finally winning the war against lice. By de-lousing the men as they come in, washing and cutting their hair and boiling clothes and bedding, we've nearly eliminated lice, ticks, and fleas. At no cost to the army."

"On the contrary. I received word you and the *Times* fund are to be fully paid back. Orders from the top."

"And a better investment you couldn't make, sir!"

He opened his mouth. He closed it. He opened it again. "Word has been getting back to England that you're supplying things you have no business supplying. Spoiling the brutes. The army issues everything its troops require. Everything! You're putting the army in a bad light."

"I'm sorry you feel that way. Apparently there is a breakdown between the warehouse and the ward. Supplies are not reaching the men who need them. Often the supplies are not in stock. You must order all your supplies out of England. That imposes delay. I simply send Mr. MacDonald half a mile into the city. No delay. I am not usurping your authority, Doctor. I am only helping."

"Why? Why do you insist on meddling?"

"Because when a man is cold and lice-ridden and sick, he needs blankets and medical supplies

immediately. Now. God cares for every man under your authority, Doctor. So do I."

"You're being sentimental about a horde of
creatures more animal than human."

"That's the prevailing opinion of the common
soldier, I realize."

"You're misguided. You understand nothing at
all about soldiers. But I know better than to think
you'll end your meddling."

"Rest assured, Doctor, neither shall I willfully
do violence to any regulation."

He snorted. He fumed. He left.

Sigma leaned in the kitchenette doorway and
watched him go. "Perhaps, Flo, you shouldn't make
him angry. He just might be powerful enough to
get us all sent home."

"Not so long as Sidney Herbert is Secretary of
War." She stood up and stretched. She had sat
quite still as Dr. Menzies ranted. She learned long
ago from Parthe's temper tantrums how best to
meet that sort of storm and fury. But being so still
made her stiff.

She had in her mind a list of things that must be
done to improve conditions here. When new sick
and wounded were coming in, neither she nor anyone else had time for frills. She and her nurses ate
meals—such as they were—on the run. They
might spend eight hours straight on their knees
dressing wounds. During the worst times Flo might
not sleep for twenty-four hours running.

But today, for the first time in a long time, she
could pursue another item on her mental list. She
would start with B ward at this end.

She entered the long hall through the doors at the near end. Those wooden shelves, those Turkish divans, lined both walls. Most of the sick soldiers, though, lay with their feet pointed toward the center of the room, mattress next to mattress next to mattress on the cold floor.

At the far end, a door led out to a tower that formed a corner of the building. There were supposed to be toilets in the towers, but the plumbing and pipes were all stopped. The men used large wooden tubs instead. The tubs would probably have worked all right, except that the orderlies never emptied them.

Flo cleared her throat and caught the eye of a passing orderly. "I understand it's one of the orderlies' duties to keep the toilet tub emptied. A distasteful job but a necessary one."

"With respect, mum, you can't give me orders. I take all my orders from the doctors."

"So do I. I'm not asking you to do a thing, young man. Just reminding you, friend to friend."

"Yes'm." He looked at her warily and went on his way.

Quietly she walked the length of the ward. Silently she stood beside the tub. Casually she folded her arms. And she waited.

Every time the orderly glanced at her he saw her eyes fixed upon him. He left; but eventually he had to come back in. Fifteen minutes later he summoned a buddy to help, and together they emptied the tub.

She smiled. "The floor is dreadfully untidy here. Shall I—"

"We'll get it," he grumped.

"Thank you, gentlemen." She walked out of the ward and on to the next. By nightfall she had seen to the emptying of most of the building's tubs. Was it her imagination or were the orderlies becoming more cooperative?

That night Flo was restless. She picked up her lamp—*her* lamp, for Mr. Ward still provided no lamps—and walked out into the dark and silent hallways. Without really thinking about what she was doing, she strolled down to Dr. McGrigor's ward.

Cautiously, quietly, she pushed open the door at this end of the long, cold ward. The darkness within had a voice; she could hear it. Rustling. Faint rustling, so constant it was almost a toneless drone. She stepped inside, holding her lamp high.

Rats! Hundreds of dark rats—a whole floor full of rats—a whole ward full of rats—scurried in all directions. In moments they had disappeared under the Turkish divans lining the walls.

Someone whispered from one of the beds. She walked over to the left, her lamp in front of her. There he was—a blond young man with his blanket all wrapped close around him.

He smiled. "The look on y'r face, mum; ye didn't know about the rats, aye?"

"I didn't know about the rats."

"They're not so bad. Gotta keep your blanket tucked in tight so they can't nibble your toes. And they kill the cockroaches."

"The cock—How useful of them!"

"Ain't it, though." He frowned. "Mum? I was the one lost part of a leg, remember?"

"I remember you, yes."

"Tell me true. Ye think I'm gonna live through this?"

"There is no doctor here better than McGrigor. You'll be on your way home to Yorkshire soon."

"How'd ye know I'm a Yorkshireman?"

"I've a friend with an accent much like yours."

Richard Monckton Milnes. She could be married to him now. She could be sitting beside him entertaining some of the world's brightest minds. She could be living a life of ease, surrounded by wealth. That's what Parthe was doing, and Mama. And Richard. No. This was her world, not that one. Not that one anymore. She thought a brief moment about his warm smile and gentle touch and forcefully shoved Richard out of mind.

"Good night, soldier." She rose and, with a smile, walked on.

Deep shadows swam along the walls behind her. She walked through the corner tower and into the next ward. The towers still smelled terribly. The tubs were being emptied regularly now; they shouldn't be this bad.

Four miles she walked, four miles of wards. With her fascination for numbers and figures, she had tallied it up, just for curiosity's sake. Some of the hundreds of men who were alive as she passed by tonight would be dead by morning. Over half of all who came here died. Over half!

Florence Nightingale was superintendent of nursing. That was all. She could not give orders, except to the nurses under her. She could not force changes. And what hurt more, she could not improve the figures and hold back the wave of death in this hellish place. Perhaps no one could. Perhaps this horror must simply go on and on and on until the war ended, no one knew when. And that troubled her most of all.

Horror upon horror. There were no longer enough strong soldiers to bury the British dead. Hired Turkish workers dumped bodies into shallow pits dug near the barracks. When the pits were full to ground level they would pile loose dirt on the grave and commence to dig the next. This was even worse than it sounds today, because in Flo's day people considered a proper, formal Christian burial extremely important.

Poor Flo. It was her nature—in her very bones —to correct every wrong she saw. In the Scutari hospitals she saw plenty of wrongs. What she didn't see was that already she was correcting many of them. She and Mr. MacDonald were doing a better job than either of them realized.

But the death rate wasn't going down. All these improvements weren't helping a bit, it seemed. They were; it just didn't seem so at the time. She kept records, added up deaths, and balanced the deaths against admissions. The winter eased up, both in the Crimea where the soldiers fought and in Scutari in Turkey. The worst was over. Even so, men were still dying by the dozens.

Things were about to change, though. Sidney Herbert was sending out a sanitation committee to investigate conditions at Scutari. They were not soldiers, not under orders from the Army; and yet they could order that changes be made if they found conditions that needed changing. Help, at last, was on the way!

7

The Commission and the Chef

March 1855

A rusty freighter lay out in the strait. With no care shown at all, sick and wounded soldiers were being lowered over the side into caiques. Like a trail of ants between the sink and the sugar bowl, the broken, crooked line of boats bobbed between ship and shore. On the shaky pier, men too weak to walk were dumped onto mules, to jerk and slide their way up the track. Those too weak to ride were carried on litters by local Turkish porters who couldn't care less what they carried. Freight? Supplies? Injured human beings? They received the same *piastres*, regardless.

From the gate, Flo watched the first of the procession approaching. She stepped back inside. "Here they come. Mary Roberts, your crew is up first. Sister Goodman, yours is next. Jane Evans's crew will keep things humming in the wards."

Flo felt a flush of pride. The processing of new patients was nowhere near what it ought to be yet, but things were improving. A doctor usually saw each man promptly. All but the worst cases were bathed and deloused. Each fellow's hair was cut and his filthy clothes replaced by a clean shirt. He was laid on a clean mattress (well, actually, not very often; that part still needed work) with a pillow and blanket. If he had no tin plate and eating utensils, they could be provided within a day or so. If he needed a basin or some special thing, he usually got it.

And still the death rate soared. *Why?*

Flo watched a few moments to make certain everything was going smoothly. Then she dived in to help. She was on her knees instantly, cutting away ruined clothing. So much of nursing was done on the knees!

"Miss Nightingale?" Aged Jane Evans was tapping her on the shoulder. "I've a bit of a problem; perhaps y'd help?"

Flo left the work to a Sellonite nurse and followed Jane out into the hall. Here were two of Flo's best nurses, looking sullen.

"These two were fighting, mum," Jane explained. "Nearly come to blows, they did."

"Surely you both know better. On duty?"

Two pairs of eyes studied the floor.

"You." Flo pointed at random. "Explain."

The girl turned blue eyes from the floor to Flo. "Mum, I've a patient more than likely to see home again, but hers is near dead. Not much hope for 'm. Mine deserves to be in the middle, not hers!"

"That's not it at all!" The other piped up, her fear suddenly gone. "She's sweet on him, is all. A favorite. Well, mine's a favorite, too, and just as likely to live."

"The middle of what?"

"The middle of the ward. Away from the death beds."

"Death beds." Flo stared at Jane. "Death beds?"

"Ye don't know about the death beds?" Jane shrugged. "The ones at the ends of the wards next to the towers. There be certain beds near the tubs and towers, that whoever's put in them dies. Every one. We try to put the worst cases on the ends and the healthiest—not the best word to use, but ye get my meaning—in the middle, where they're most likely to survive."

To decide which claim lacked merit would take too long. Flo would nip the problem at its root. "You both know that arguing and fighting is unthinkable. You'll work down here in Receiving. Jane, send two Sellonites up to the ward in their place. She turned on her heel. "Death beds!" And marched down the hall toward Dr. McGrigor's cubicle. He'd know about this, surely.

She stopped cold. What was this? Whatever was this?!

In the gate came a Frenchman. He was singing a song in a rich French accent—but even had his mouth been closed he would have been a Frenchman. His clothes, the lively spring in his step—only a Frenchman.

Behind him, with a stolid dignity that made butlers look like rugby players, strode a gentleman. The man was dressed in the very crispest, sharpest of formal attire. Here was a gentleman's gentleman who was a perfect gentleman. He carried a satchel and writing case.

The Frenchman spotted Flo instantly and came bounding over. "What blessing! I arrive in zis gray tomb of a building and what first meets my eyes? The fairest of flowers, a lily of rarest perfection! Mademoiselle, allow me to introduce myself. Alexis Soyer, at your beck and service." He grabbed her hand and with a wild flourish kissed it as he bowed. It was a long time since anyone greeted her with such Gallic enthusiasm. Flo realized she had rather missed it.

"I'm Florence Nightingale. I've heard your name."

"Reform Club, perhaps. I am ze chef in charge."

"Of course. And what is the finest chef in Europe doing here in a British army hospital?"

"A grand experiment, Mademoiselle. Panmure himself, he sends me with his blessing. I volunteer, and he says 'yes! Let us attempt zis grand experiment!' *Voici!* I am here."

"What experiment?"

"At Reform Club, I serve ze finest foods to perfection. For a man of my skill, zat is not difficult. A bit of zis, a bit of zat. And who tastes it? A few gentlemen of high rank. Ah, but to prepare ze exquisite dish for thousands—what ze challenge!"

"You want to cook for an army hospital?"

"*Oui!*"

"And make it taste as good as the food at the Reform Club, for which you are famous?"

"*Mais oui!*"

"Do you know how they cook here?"

"*Non,* but I—"

"The orderly for each ward brings a joint of meat down to the kitchen. He marks it as his own any way he can; some drive a nail into their meat. Another might tie a rag around it. Then each man throws his meat into great cooking pots."

"*Non!*"

"*Oui.* There is precious little fuel for cooking. Green wood, which produces more smoke than heat. The pots never really reach boiling. They lie there and simmer. When the cook decides the meat has been cooking long enough, he dumps the pots and the orderlies take their meat. The first into the pot is fairly cooked. The last in comes out nearly raw. The orderlies cut up the joints and carry them to their wards."

"But ze meat must get cold so quickly."

"It does. And the raw meat is bad for men suffering cholera. Their body can't digest it. Horribly painful cramps."

"But vegetables . . . just ze vegetables for such ill . . ."

"Rarely any vegetables. Dried peas sometimes."

"Then my work is cut up for me!"

"So to speak."

Major Sillery called from his office door. "Miss Nightingale? Some people here who asked to meet you. Ah." He came out into the hall. "Monsieur Soyer?"

"Ze very same." Most Englishmen would shake hands. The Frenchman bowed from the waist.

Major Sillery motioned to an aide behind him. "Show this gentleman around—the kitchen in particular. Miss Nightingale?"

Flo followed him into his office.

Major Sillery waved a hand around. "Doctor John Sutherland, Robert Rawlinson, Doctor Milroy, uh—" He licked his lips. "And these three gentlemen are sanitary inspectors from the borough of Liverpool. They've had excellent results there, and Lord Panmure felt they would be of value here."

This was the sanitary committee Sidney had promised. Flo smiled and curtsied. She'd not remember all those names any better than Major Sillery could. "Gentlemen. The very smell of this place tells me you'll be of help. My nurses and I are at your disposal."

Dr. Sutherland bowed. He was English, of course. "Let us not tarry, Major. Perhaps a tour of inspection—?"

"Certainly."

No one told Flo not to join the group. She tagged along, staying on the edges, lest the Major notice her and suggest some duty she ought to be attending to. The superintendent of nurses had no business butting into the sanitary commission's affairs.

They walked the wards almost as Flo herself did each night. But they carried no lamps, for it was day. Nor did they bother to cover all four miles of corridors. They discussed the corner towers in hushed tones.

The Major led them out into the abandoned courtyard, which formed the center of this huge box of a building. Trash, weeds, a dead cat, dried bushes—it might have served once as a pleasant view from the inside windows of the wards. Now, though, it was as dead as the unfortunate soldiers so often carried out.

One of the commissioners pointed to the privies dug right beside the great water tanks. They all nodded and made notes. Flo pressed her lips together. Were these men going to be gentlemen who would wag their heads, make a few suggestions and then sail home to comfortable old England?

"Look here." Dr. Sutherland was on his knees by a small window in the foundation. With a board he smashed in the filthy window.

The others gathered around him. Flo didn't have to look. She could smell it.

Dr. Sutherland stood up. "Major, the sewer system here is completely clogged. The basement, the foundation, is filled with sewage. It's in the walls. The fumes are being sucked up through the towers. I'll wager it's a major source of your illness."

Death beds.

One of the Liverpool inspectors turned to Flo. "What color is your water here?"

"Brownish. Grayish brownish, actually."

"Particulates?"

"Bits of things floating in it? Definitely."

Major Sillery frowned. "Miss Nightingale, shouldn't you be supervising the care of incoming patients?"

Ah, well. It had lasted longer than she thought it would. "Of course, sir. Excuse me, gentlemen?"

As she turned and headed back toward the big inside doors, she heard one of the inspectors call,

"Let's trace the water source back, gentlemen." And off they went again. If only these men's enthusiasm for the task continued, something good might come of the commission after all.

She was almost instantly back on her knees. More immediate necessities pushed the commission to the back of her mind. M. Soyer she practically forgot. It was late evening before the last of the new arrivals was tucked away in a ward.

She knew now pretty much who was here and what their problems were. The worst cases she would nurse herself. She had promised four men she would write to their families for them; she must do that yet tonight, for she'd have no time tomorrow. The last of the nurses to leave the wards (as always), she trudged up the stairs toward quarters.

And here was Major Sillery, headed for his quarters. "Good night, Miss Nightingale."

"Major." She paused and smiled. "You look so very weary. The commission must have led you a merry chase."

"I should have let you come along as they followed out our water source. From the tanks to ditches; they had to see every inch of it."

"And their findings?"

"I admit they found a few major problems. We discovered a dead horse in one of the service ditches. The water supply is being filtered through a dead horse."

"It doesn't surprise me, actually. The smell of it—"

"That was easy enough taken care of; remove the horse. You can't imagine all the other changes they want made, though, and right now, too! And I'm under direct orders to cooperate. And then there's that Frenchman, what's his name—"

"Soyer. Alexis Soyer. He appears a clown, Major, but his reputation as a chef is without equal. If anyone can make the food of Scutari edible, he'll do it."

"These are *soldiers*, Miss Nightingale! Not gentlemen! They are common ruffians. Scum."

"Dying scum, Major." She got an idea. "The army has quite an investment in each of her soldiers—training, transportation. Many of the men we save can be returned to the front to do battle again. Look on this hospital as protecting the army's investment. Whether they be lords or ruffians, they're worth money on the battlefield."

"I hadn't quite thought of it that way. But gourmet food?"

" 'Twas Napoleon a hundred years ago who said an army travels on its stomach. Good food increases the value of the investment."

The Major studied her a moment. "You're trying to flummox me, Miss Nightingale. And I'm just weary enough to let you. Good night."

"Good night, sir." And Flo continued upstairs. There was work waiting there.

You cannot imagine how much good the sanitary commission achieved. Using local workers, they drained the sewer system and made it right. They whitewashed the walls of the wards to seal out noxious smells. They had those Turkish divans torn out as the first step in getting rid of the rats. They cleaned up the water supply.

And M. Soyer? He bounded from day into day absolutely bristling with ideas. He invented a teapot big enough to make tea for fifty patients at a time. He invented ovens for baking bread and rolls. He overhauled the kitchen and refused to boil any food. He trained soldiers to be cooks.

Not the least modest or retiring, he took great pride in his cooking accomplishments. His pride was so great, in fact, that before the war ended he invited the most important British officers in Turkey to a banquet—and served them hospital food!

The military leaders didn't much appreciate him. Pampering the brutes, they said. Ah, but what did the pampered brutes, the soldiers, think? When M. Soyer and his assistants carried containers of soup through the wards, the patients cheered them three times three. That's what the brutes thought.

The improved care, the improved food, the improved sanitation; what did it all accomplish? Flo kept careful figures. Studying her numbers, she was the first to see it: During the first three months of 1855, for every hundred men who entered the hospital, more than four hundred died! But by summer, that tragic, cold, death rate number—415—had shrunk down to 2.

8

From Frying Pan to Fire

May 1855

There was Robert, all crumpled into a ball, asleep beside her door. He claimed to be eighteen, the minimum age for army service. If he was thirteen, that was years more than he looked. He must have been poorly fed to be so small and scrawny for his age, whatever it was. Huge hands and feet and skinny arms and legs gave him a clumsy look. He was really not the least clumsy. When asleep, he slept like the earth itself. When awake, he made that whirlwind M. Soyer look like siesta time in Madrid.

Flo cleared her throat. "Good evening, Robert. It's time."

He stirred, grinned, and leaped to his feet. "I'll get your lamp!" Did scientists dream of unlocking the secret of the sun's energy? And did they dream of harnessing that energy? If they were to harness Robert's energy, they wouldn't need the sun.

He popped out into the hall, with one hand shielding the lamp flame from the wind of haste. He forged ahead and matched his stride to the steps he heard behind him.

Dr. McGrigor stepped out into the hall and closed the door of his ward behind him. Once upon a time, when Flo first arrived here, he had bounced almost as much as M. Soyer. These last six months had made an old man of him. "Miss Nightingale, good evening. Hello, Robert."

"Doctor, sir."

"So Miss Nightingale has asked you to carry her lamp during her rounds, did she?"

"I volunteered, sir." And the boy grinned as wide as Salisbury Plain.

"Good man." He looked at Flo. "What's this about a reading room? And a postal money transfer?"

"Lord Paulet says what all the other high muck-a-mucks say—I'm spoiling the brutes. But he gave permission for a reading room. We'll build a shack for it between the general hospital and the barracks hospital here. I'll stock it myself with writing paper, pens, and ink—that sort of thing—maps, newspapers, and magazines. Patients who can walk can sit there and read, or write home. Do you realize that in this hospital no patient has a flat surface—except the floor—upon which to write a letter?"

"They'll steal your writing paper and sell it for grog."

"That's what Lord Paulet said, too. I think better. But he flat out denied my request for the postal service."

"You actually think these soldiers would send money home? They drink it. The whole payroll goes into the booze mills."

"Lord Panmure said that, too. If the government hadn't changed—if Sidney were still the Secretary at War—we'd have those things now. But Panmure is harder to convince."

"And you think the men would send money home if they could."

"Every Friday afternoon I receive at the warehouse any man who wants to send his pay home. I record amounts and destinations, then send it in one big check to my Uncle Samuel. He sends it on."

"And I'll bet you've handled fifty, maybe a hundred pounds that way."

"A thousand pounds a month."

Dr. McGrigor stared at her a moment. "Now I hear you're considering sailing up to the Crimea itself to raise a fuss in the hospitals there. Don't you ever relax?"

"You've been talking to Dr. Hall's associates. Dr. Hall opposes everything I hope to do. He doesn't like female army nurses." She laughed. "Praise God the place is in good order now. Sigma can handle the correspondence and free gift stores. The nurses know their duties. It's a good time for me to break away for a few weeks. The death rate in the field hospitals is nearly as high as it was last winter. If I can force any changes at all, 'twill be for the better. 'Twill save lives."

" 'Scuse me, sir." Robert beamed like a light-house. "I'll be going, too, as Miss Nightingale's assistant. And so's M. Soyer."

"Indeed. Quite a party. God bless your journey, Florence Nightingale."

"And God bless your work, good doctor."

He went his way. She paused on hers to turn and watch him. He walked hunch-shouldered now, and shuffling. He was a weary, weary man.

Miserable a sailor as she was, Flo almost welcomed the steamship voyage from Scutari across the Black Sea to Balaclava. It was a most welcome rest. At Scutari, in addition to all her nursing duties—she still took the worst cases herself—she ordered most of the supplies, for poor Mr. Ward simply could not make the warehouse function properly.

And the writing! She wrote long reports to Sidney Herbert. She wrote letters to officials. She wrote letters for her nurses who could not read and write. She wrote letters home for the men. She sat at bedsides as soldiers died, then wrote the sad news to their families, telling how bravely the young men passed on.

And now she was sailing into more work and more grief for herself, from the frying pan into the fire. The field hospitals in the Crimea were a shambles. Perhaps even she could not put them to rights. Was Dr. McGrigor right? Perhaps she should simply rest a while.

But then she thought about the hundreds and hundreds of needless, senseless deaths, deaths that were happening right now in the Crimea because conditions there were still as bad as they had been at Scutari. No. She could not rest.

Nothing could appear more peaceful than Balaclava Harbor as their ship sloshed and waddled her way to the dock. No caiques here, no rickety wooden pier. Steep, huddled hills shouldered each other and crowded against the shore. A city of army tents and canvas marquees filled the waterfront. They stretched up and out along the slopes beyond.

No place—not anywhere the eye rested—could Flo see a tree or bush. Barren rocks and some grass, that was all.

Robert popped out of nowhere and pushed up to the rail to the right of her. "What's the bad smell, Mum, d'ja know?"

"Smells like dead something, but I—" She stopped.

Robert had clamped his hand over his mouth. Silently he pointed to the murky water below. There was a human arm wedged in the pilings a few feet below the surface.

M. Soyer stepped in beside Flo on her left. "Body parts, *oui*, Ma'amzelle. I ask ze captain what is ze smell. The field hospital, she dumps all her throwaway in the harbor he says. Ze sanitary commission is begin ze clean up. Ship captains, as all sea persons, zey are very superstitious, *oui?* Don't like to haul up ze anchor and find such parts tangled in ze chain."

"An understandable aversion. The whole harbor here reeks of garbage and decay. It looks so peaceful, but it—" She wagged her head. "Time to go ashore and pay our respects to Lord Raglan."

Robert's eyes grew wide. "I'll meet the great man, too? Why he conducts the whole war, just about."

"Just about." Flo smiled. "He's an old friend of mine."

The great man was not in.

"He'll be back tomorrow, milady." A junior officer bowed, all starch and formality. "If you've a few hours, we'd like to give you a tour of the mortar battery. It's of military interest, of course, but it's also a lovely view of the whole countryside. I understand you ride. My wife's sidesaddle is at your disposal if you wish."

"Yes. Why thank you. We'd like that very much."

The mare provided her was a charming little bay, all spice and vinegar, as Papa loved to say. Papa. If only he could see her now; he'd be shocked. He raised a high society lady, a delicate flower born to grace parlors and make polite conversation. Now here was his delicate flower cavorting around a war zone, doing a nursing job not even the men could handle.

Charles rode a slow and rather artless old horse, and that was good; Charles was a rather artless rider. M. Soyer elected to walk ("I will ride on ze good two legs ze way God intends a man should travel"). Robert kept up with him, but it wasn't easy. M. Soyer and waif bounded along together, two small boys turned loose to explore a great, wonderful world.

Those leaves in the rocks, all yellow and wilted —Flo knew them. Of course! Crocus and hyacinth. Spring blooms. In English gardens they were carefully cultivated. Here in the Crimea they grew wild. So did the lilies, and they were blooming now.

They scrambled up a steep wagon track and topped out on a rocky ridge. What a view! Hills rolled north nearly to the horizon; they flattened to a straight line in the distant haze. There was Sebastopol over there, the fortress held by the enemy, the Russians. From this distance no enemy could be seen. Behind them over there, the Black Sea stretched halfway to forever.

"Why are there no trees or bushes?"

"Our troops ripped them out for fuel last winter. Roots and all." The young officer shifted in his saddle. "Bad time, Mum. All the horses starved; the men were hardly any better off. A storm destroyed much materiel that was never replaced. Many died because of the cold, bad weather or cholera."

"So zis is ze mortar battery." M. Soyer had forged ahead. He and Robert stood amid uniformed soldiers beside huge, ugly guns with giant maws. Then he came bounding over to Flo. "Ma'amzelle, would she please dismount a moment? A favor to me, *oui?*"

A titter of recognition rippled through the artillerymen. They must have recognized Flo; they broke out in a cheer, three times three. Flo's mare danced in place as Robert hung onto her bravely. The horse's eyes rolled back so far the whites showed.

Flo was not accustomed to cheers, either. They made her head ring. Her eyes felt burny and tight.

M. Soyer escorted Flo to one of those great guns and perched her on top of it. He stepped back and gestured grandly with sweeping arm. "Behold, zis amiable lady sitting fearlessly upon ze terrible instrument of war! Behold ze heroic daughter of England, ze soldier's friend."

Another wave of cheers rolled forth. Robert clung gamely to the nervous mare.

More a schoolboy than a warrior, a young soldier bashfully presented Flo with a lily. So did another. And another. "Choose which you prefer," they asked her.

Flo knew an opportunity for diplomacy when she saw it. "I do so like flowers! Might I keep them all, please?" She scooped them into her arms.

They could not return to Balaclava a moment too soon. Smelly and revolting though the harbor might be, there she could board the ship and rest her thumping head; she could get out of the sun and get rid of this headache.

They clattered into Balaclava, and she retired to her quarters. A night's sleep did nothing for her headache; if anything, it was worse. In a sort of fog, she toured the general hospital. What she had heard was right. The superintendent, a seventy-year-old lady who liked to gossip over tea, would have to be replaced.

They climbed the hill to Castle Hospital. Flo liked this place even less. It was nothing more than huts and tents.

M. Soyer went off to invade hospital kitchens. He left his secretary with Flo. She welcomed help. The man could take notes, and she need do nothing more than sit in the salon of the ship and try somehow to remain alert.

The secretary ushered her to a moldy-smelling davenport and sat down beside her, his notebook open. "Before we see Miss Weare, have you any preliminary opinions, Madame, as to what needs correction?"

"The patients here are unwashed. The nurses should be keeping them clean. Their dressings and bandages haven't been changed recently, probably since they were first applied. Dressings and bandaging must be kept fresh to reduce infection and lice. Their bedding should be changed regularly; it's not been. All hard work, and all necessary if the patient is to recover. But not the sort of thing Miss Weare and her nursing ladies like to do. So it's not being done. There's your problem."

"Indeed, Madame." His voice was becoming distant, hollow. She wished he would stop addressing her as Madame. Properly, that title was for a married woman. Of course, in a sense, Flo was married to her work. It was her life, her love, as much as a husband is to a devoted woman. What was Richard Monckton Milnes doing now?

Then the secretary was shaking her and shouting at her. Didn't he know her head pounded and his loud voice made her ears ring? The salon here was very cold. Perhaps they should go to the deck for the interview with Miss Weare, out in the sun. No. The smell was too bad out there. Perhaps—

Why didn't M. Soyer's secretary stop shouting? Why was Flo suddenly staring at the ceiling? Many voices, many hands buzzed all around her. She recognized one or two of the doctors. She certainly knew Charles, but he didn't answer the questions she asked.

She heard Robert sobbing.

She heard a man's voice near her ear saying, "Crimean fever. The worst case I've seen in a long while."

Who had Crimean fever? Flo couldn't remember the name of the person she would be interviewing shortly. She floated, she felt perfectly miserable. Sleep kept forcing itself on her. She kept resisting. She had too much to do to sleep.

Too much to do.

Flo never did things by half, as you well know. Nor did she get sick by halves. She lay fevered for weeks. She tossed and turned; the only way they could keep her quiet was to provide her a pen and paper and let her write. What she wrote, of course, was practically nonsense.

They had to move her from the general hospital near shore to the Castle Hospital on the hill because the smell by the harbor was too strong. Through a clammy rain, strong men carried her in a litter, and they wept. Little Robert wept, too, frustrated because he was not strong enough to help carry the litter, or tall enough to carry the umbrella held above her head.

They cut off her hair, her lovely, long auburn hair, because that's what you did in those days when a person had fever. When Lord Raglan finally got to Balaclava to see her, she was in her right mind again but so weak she could not speak above a whisper.

She would have to return to Scutari to recuperate. Dr. Hall himself had her put aboard a ship. Only at the last moment did Charles discover the ship was not stopping at Scutari; Flo's enemies were sending her straight to England! Hastily Charles arranged another passage, on a private steam yacht, and she arrived safely at Scutari.

She was months getting well enough to return to work. Even so, she never fully recovered.

The reading room worked out splendidly, and that pleased her very much. No one stole paper. No one talked loudly or caused a fuss. It was always crowded.

Eventually Flo's other idea won out, too. The army set up postal outlets so the men could send their pay home. The project was an enormous success! The next year she talked the army into providing classes for the common soldiers there at Scutari. Teachers and professors came out from England and taught standing-room-only crowds—another great success.

But the greatest success of all was one Flo never really appreciated. She knew how crude British soldiers could be, but she also knew how courteous and courageous they were. Through her efforts with the classes, the reading room, the postal service, she showed the world what she had always known about her soldiers.

And that was one of her greatest victories: The British soldier's officers began to see him in a new way. His country began to treat him better. Just as Flo would change forever the image of the nurse, so she changed the image of the soldier. Never again would the British soldier be seen as a brute and a ruffian. From the Crimean war emerged a new British soldier, a respected hero.

It was the soldiers themselves, though, who returned to England trumpeting the fame of the real hero of Crimea—Florence Nightingale.

9

Going Home

Spring 1856

Dead-axle baggage cart. That's what Colonel McMurdo called it. A cart was a very small wagon to be drawn by mule or horse, used to haul army baggage. Simple enough. But Flo now learned what dead-axle means—no springs.

Every carriage she had ever ridden in had been fitted with steel springs or leather thoroughbraces to take the jolts out of travel—until now. Every time the baggage cart's wheels clunked down into a hole or rut, the whole cart dropped out from under her. With each rock and bump in the road she popped straight up. And these Crimean roads were all ruts and rocks.

No matter. When problems in her legs made horseback too painful, they had given her a mule cart. It had tipped over and dumped her out. This vehicle, though, was solid and sturdy. She could count on it to stay right side up. And unlike the mule cart, it was covered with canvas over great hoops. The snow and icy rain could not reach her here. Would this miserable weather never sweeten up?

She who hated cold was plagued by it. The nurses' rooms at Scutari were cold all winter long. The charcoal brazier from France gave her headaches; she ended up using it for a table. The little stove wouldn't draw properly. And that was in Turkey. Turkey is supposed to be a hot country. Now here in the Crimea, the cold was even worse.

The rain dwindled to a coarse mist as her shaggy little horse picked its way down the track. Deep gloom darkened the trail. The sun had quit the field, to shine on more peaceful lands across the world.

Was that cheering up ahead? It was certainly noise. The mist glowed orange beyond the hill. A fire, perhaps—? Flo urged her little horse from a plod to a jog.

The glow came not from a wildfire but from a hundred smoking burning torches in the headquarters compound. As her jouncy little cart lurched into the yard, a grinning cavalryman clattered by. He fired his gun into the dark sky, and Flo's horse jumped and rolled its eyes. She trusted her own legs farther than she trusted this horse, however sturdy the cart might be. She hopped out.

Out of nowhere a happy lance corporal grabbed her for a hug. He leaped back gasping, embarrassed, and snatched his hat off his head. "Sorry, Mum! So sorry! Didn't know 'twas yerself, Miss Nightingale, or I never . . ." The grin came back. " 'Tis over, Mum! The war's over and done!"

"Truce?"

"And not a minute too soon, aye? They proclaimed the peace as of April twenty-nine, but 'twill take 'em a while to work out the details, they say. All'a same, the shooting's done."

"Cause for rejoicing, indeed. Carry on, Corporal, as you no doubt will."

She abandoned the baggage cart to wherever the little horse chose to take it. She stood still for a moment, fighting to keep her bearings and dignity in the midst of the chaos. Men yelled and fired guns. They greeted each other laughing. They ran to and fro and, more dangerous, rode fidgety horses back and forth through the compound. More torches flared alight.

She worked her way across the compound to Colonel McMurdo's qarters.

"Come in, Miss Nightingale!" The tightness in the colonel's face had loosened considerably, but Flo could still see the bitterness there. He was smiling. "You heard the news, no doubt." He waved toward a chair. "Be seated. You know the Major here, and my aide, of course. Do join us."

"I join you with pleasure. Never a bad thing to honor, peace."

"Many things to be ironed out yet, but the fighting is declared done. No more enemy. We and the Czar's Hussars may ride together to the hounds, for all that the powers-that-be care."

"No more casualties."

Flo smiled. "I doubt the revelry outside will permit us that luxury, Major. Men are men, at peace or at war."

"And what next for you, Miss Nightingale?" The colonel settled into a chair beside her.

She shrugged. "I must send home my nurses as the need for them slackens. The women here I'll handle personally. The nurses at Scutari I must deal with by letter." She wagged her head. "More correspondence."

"Which reminds me. I have several pieces for you in the military post and some private letters."

"News from Scutari, I trust. They keep me well informed."

"Your nurses. You don't know what splendid reports we get from Scutari; and of course, we've seen it ourselves here. All of them ministering angels."

Flo laughed out loud. "Such unusual angels! Jane Evans, for example—an old woman who spent her whole life until now herding pigs. And yet she's turned out to be one of our best. I hear she's adopted a buffalo calf. I'll arrange for the buffalo to go home with her."

"Hardly a dignified image."

"A small reward for service. And Miss Tebbuts. She's been so overworked. I'll ask Mama to let her rest at my home; she has no other place. Perhaps her aged mother can join her, too." Flo stood up. "That is what I'll be doing next, Major. I must deal with each, one by one, every woman. I want no one accidentally thrown off like an old shoe."

Outside, bedlam erupted anew. A horse whinnied, terrified. Men cried out. Flo caught the colonel's eye, and he wagged his head. *Hopeless.* She smiled and nodded and stepped out into the riotous night.

The peace treaty was finally signed on March 30. Still, it took Flo until late June to close down the last of the Crimean facilities. With scarce a look behind her, she sailed home to Scutari.

Scutari? Home? It almost seemed so. There was the hulking stone box perched on its hill, waiting. She bobbed toward its pier in a gaily painted caique. But it had changed. It no longer glowered, dismal and threatening. No more smell. No more death within its walls. It simply sat there, blank and listless, like a huge square period at the end of a long and nightmarish sentence.

As she stepped from boat to pier she heard a familiar voice up the hill: "Hurry! A boat is here!"

Here came Margaret Goodman, her Sellonite nurses marching smartly behind her. Although the hot summer sun burned bright, they wore their black wool habits just as they always did.

Flo smiled. "Godspeed, Margaret, and God bless you."

"And you, Miss Florence." She sniffled, but she was smiling.

"Are there many left up there?"

"Very few. No new cases. Most of them are up and around. They'll be leaving before long."

"Strange, isn't it, how the place tugs at one? I hear that Mother Bermondsey also went home with tears in her eyes."

"A short time ago, aye. Ah, Miss Florence, what a time it was! Never before and never to be again."

"No, Margaret, I'm afraid there will be a time again, somewhere. You saved many lives. For that, be glad. But the next time, as many lives again will be lost because of man's stupidity. The way of doing things hasn't changed. It's still there, ready to send young men to their deaths at the next call to war."

The sister wagged her head sadly. "When you came you were so hopeful. And now you're so bitter."

"Bitter? No, disappointed. You and I have seen what few people on earth have ever seen. Certainly the men who declare wars have never seen it. In six months all this will have been forgotten, and those men will have died in vain."

Margaret picked up her bag. "God does not forget. And God loves. No man dies in vain before God. We must go now." Her lip trembled. Quite probably she had been intending a simple handshake. Suddenly, though, the black-clad arms stretched out and around and wrapped Flo in a tight hug. When the sister at last let go her cheeks were wet, her eyes bleary, her nose clogged and slurpy. With a forced little smile she turned and hurried down the pier.

Flo watched the sisters clamber into the bright caique. They passed bags and satchels from hand to hand. The boat left the dock and bobbed slowly out to the waiting steamer.

Flo waited. She hoped Margaret's firm faith would somehow rub off on her along with the hug and lift her out of her sadness. No such thing. She started up the rutted track.

After two years—after the whole war and despite Flo's begging—the track was still just as rutted and narrow as ever. It had not changed.

The Coffee House was deserted. Its door swung, creaking and clapping, on the warm summer breeze. Here she had proved that the British soldier was a man to be respected and trusted.

She walked on through the silent wing, her heels ticking, and out into the great inner courtyard. Rubbish was starting to pile up again. A dead cat lay near the water tanks.

She sighed. "Nothing has been accomplished, really." She let her aching thoughts drift. "No, Margaret. In all this waste and useless death, not a thing has been accomplished."

Poor Flo. She was wrong, of course. You see, that was the way she was; if a cause didn't end up exactly the way she wanted it to, she considered it lost; that was simply the way she always looked at things. She never did realize that in that short, horrid Crimean war she personally had changed things forever.

Do you remember? When the war began, the common British soldier was considered a brute animal, to be bullied about and treated no differently than a mule. Flo showed the world the nobility, good sense, and courage of her beloved soldiers; with the coffee-house reading room, postal remittances, and classes of instruction, she single-handedly changed the way England looked at its fighting men. Ever since Florence Nightingale, England's soldiers have never lost the respect she gained for them.

But she did far more than that. Before Flo boarded that ship bound for Scutari, nursing was a dirty, distasteful job no decent English girl would want. After all, everyone thought nurses were drunkards—women with low morals. But you'll remember that right from the start she set the very highest standards for nursing and nurses at Scutari. The soldiers those nurses cared for brought their war stories home to England. They told of a new kind of nurse, a noble and respected nurse. The image of that new nurse was the image of Florence Nightingale herself—always caring, morally upright, devoted and true. The grateful soldiers remembered the thin, somber lady with the lamp as she walked the endless corridors. No more was nursing considered indecent. On her own, Florence Nightingale made nursing an honorable career.

So you see, by going to the Crimea she changed something greater than a system for doing things. She changed men's attitudes; and you will surely agree that that's the very hardest thing of all to change.

She had listened to God's call. She had done what she must, what no other proper English lady had ever done. But her service to mankind wasn't over yet. The best was yet to come.

10

The Queen's Ear

Summer 1856

The train chugged into the familiar little station, shimmied, and sighed to a halt. Flo looked out the sooty gray window. Anyone standing around? No. Good. She had told no one she was coming, but that didn't mean it would remain a secret.

She stepped into the aisle and waited as an old woman got out in front of her. The things people planned! Honestly. Any number of well-meaning but foolish people declared Flo a national hero. A committee of men, including Richard Monckton Milnes, had even read a paper in Parliament officially declaring her one. A *hero?* The heroes were those thousands of young men in mass graves, and all of them would be soon forgotten, if they weren't already. Well, let England forget about Florence Nightingale, too. Flo would not take part in their hubbub.

They wanted to welcome her back to England with a triumphal parade. They wanted to honor her with speeches. Even her own mother and sister talked about huge parties to welcome her home.

Flo moved forward and stepped down onto the platform. That was logical, come to think of it. Her mother and sister lived for big parties. Celebrate any little thing—or nothing at all—and they instantly planned a party. It was the way their minds always worked.

In letters to her before she left Scutari, they claimed they were welcoming her with open arms. They claimed they were so terribly proud of her. She thought about all those other years; the screaming, the tantrums, the hysterics; Papa running away to his club in London to hide from the uproar at home. The daughter and sister they praised so highly now was the very same woman they had shrieked at and called every name imaginable. She had not changed. If they had, it was only because public opinion had forced them to.

She had sent all her baggage down to Embley. Why did Colonel McMurdo insist that she bring that dead-axle baggage cart with her? Ah, well; if one must have a memento of the war, that was as interesting as any.

She left the village and walked familiar lanes toward Lea Hurst.

As always, the grounds were perfectly manicured. She came up the curved driveway. Why didn't she feel more at home? There on the hill stood the great house with its many windows. Her father often spoke of the matchless view from the house.

Her mother was not the first to greet her, neither was her father or her sister. The front door swung open, and a portly woman in a maid's uniform burst forth. Mrs. Watson. Here she came running down the curved driveway. Sobbing, she flung her loving arms around Flo's neck. *Now* Flo was home.

Not a thing had changed in the Nightingale family in Flo's absence. Flo had, though. She found herself pacing the floor all night, unable to sleep. She ate next to nothing; the very sight of food made her feel sick. Possibly this was some aftermath of the Crimean fever. More probably it was frustration—Flo was home, nine thousand soldiers lay rotting in unmarked graves in Turkey, and she was not doing a thing to prevent the tragedy repeating itself. Worse, she had no idea where to start doing something.

Papa declared that he simply couldn't watch her waste away and went down to Embley. Papa—hiding again. Mama absolutely *had* to know when Flo would be re-entering society, that she might begin planning social functions for her. Parthe fawned over her and hovered around her so constantly that Flo put her to work.

People had discovered Flo was home; the mail began. So Flo set Parthe to writing most of the replies. The marriage proposals, for example—Flo got lots of those. She let Parthe write the polite refusals. One fellow wanted not a wife but a donkey; he reasoned that since Flo had been in Turkey, and there were many many donkeys in Turkey, she could surely send him one.

And then there was the Nightingale Fund. Thousands of pounds donated by soldiers and private citizens lay in an account, just waiting to be used. Flo got large numbers of letters telling her how it ought—and ought not—be spent. She could clearly see that whatever she did with it would raise storms of protest from some faction or other. That fund wasn't a tool—it was a millstone around her neck.

Now here she was, coming down the stairs to greet another day. Summer would be soon gone, and she was accomplishing nothing. Nothing!

At the table by the window Mama was arranging dahlias in the blue ming vase. She smiled mechanically at Flo and Flo crossed to give her a good-morning peck on the cheek.

Parthe sat at her little writing desk. She waved a large envelope. "Here's another invitation—a banquet and plaque. The usual polite rejection?"

"Yes, please."

Parthe sniffed. "Honestly, Flo! I find your indifference to praise extraordinary."

Mrs. Watson appeared in the doorway, stiff and proper. "A messenger from the Duke of Devonshire," she announced.

Mama stood erect, just as proper. "Show him through."

It was Flo who recognized the man and crossed to greet him. She extended both hands. "Mr. Paxton. We're delighted."

"I'm honored you remember me, Miss Nightingale. The Duke's warmest greetings." He pinned a small box against his side with one elbow, took her hands in his and kissed her knuckles.

"Our warmest in return. Mama, you remember Joseph Paxton, head gardener at Chatsworth. He built the great glass house."

"Of course. Mr. Paxton." No, Mama did not in the least remember. But naturally she was the soul of politeness.

"Mrs. Watson? Tea, please." Flo gestured toward the morocco easy chair. "Do be seated, Mr. Paxton. How is the Duke?"

"In fine health. I'll convey to him your interest."

"And Chatsworth and that wonderful glass house?"

"Fine." He beamed. "I've built another, a small one with a pool, specifically for raising giant water lilies. But now, my purpose in coming. The Duke is a most ardent fan of your efforts. And he sends this remembrance." He handed her the little box.

Flo took her time opening it. "Athena. The Duke remembers Athena. How utterly lovely." She lifted out a delicate silver statue. It very touchingly resembled her little lost owl. "It's wonderful! My warmest thanks to the Duke."

"He understood that you once had a beloved pet owl."

"In the flurry of preparing to go to Turkey, Athena was accidentally locked in an attic, where she died. The only tears I shed when I left were tears for her. Odd, how much I loved the little beastie. I shall treasure this."

"I'll tell him that." Mr. Paxton whipped an envelope out of his coat. "The Duke requests your presence at a reception in your honor at Chatsworth. We'll do the glasshouse up in lights."

Flo thought briefly of that marvelous night at Chatsworth, the thousands of gleaming lamps and torches, the splendor of a giant glass building alive with tropical beauty, glowing in the darkness. And for her! It would all be for her.

"I'm so sorry I must deline. I particularly regret having to say no to such a lovely man as the Duke."

Mama and Parthe wilted like flowers left too long out of water. Mama cleared her throat. "Excuse me momentarily, Mr. Paxton; matters I must attend." She stood up.

"I'll help her." Parthe rose, too.

Mr. Paxton stood politely as they left the room, then seated himself again.

"Mr. Paxton," Flo said, "this is for the Duke's ear only. Drastic changes must be made in the system—in the machinery of war—or the disaster of Crimea will repeat itself. The newspapers have told our country about the tragic and unnecessary waste of life, and they claim it would have been far worse had I not been there."

"And it's true! You're so popular! You have immense power now!"

"Not in the right circles to get anything accomplished, don't you see? I have no influence whatever with the men who must make the changes. Perhaps I'm making a terrible mistake; I don't know. It's the road I am taking. I just don't know."

September came. Surely God would remind someone besides Flo of all those nine thousand dead. On an autumn morning when the swallows had fled and the asters were finishing their blooming, Mama as usual arranged fresh flowers on the window table. Parthe sat as usual at her writing desk, sorting through mail.

"Sir James Clark invites you to Birk Hall to..." Parthe's eyes grew wide. "Flo! This is a command appearance before the queen herself!" Her eyes narrowed. "You'd better not refuse this one! Honestly, Flo! To even think you might. . . ."

"No, I'll not refuse this one." A dream in Flo's heart suddenly promised to become reality. "A royal commission! I've been thinking such a commission would be the best way to change things. Here is its opportunity. I'll have the ear of the queen herself! I'll need facts and figures—"

"What *are* you babbling about?" Parthe stared at her.

"Parthe, the stilled voices of nine thousand are about to speak to the queen."

Once upon a time in the dim past, Flo had gotten up before breakfast to study Blue Books by candlelight. She used now what she learned then. When she and Papa rode on to Birk Hall she carried in her bag a hundred tragic secrets about to be made known. They arrived there on Monday the fifteenth. On the seventeenth they were commanded to Balmoral Castle, where Flo would meet the queen.

The great, gray granite castle, with its two massive blocks and imposing tower, ought to appear cold and forbidding. It did not. Prince Albert had purchased it as a gift for his beloved wife. He had

spent two years furnishing it in the style of the old
Scots barons who had built it. A love gift for a
queen—how could it be frightening?

That visit on a Wednesday afternoon was the
first of many visits. Flo discussed metaphysics
with Prince Albert. She talked about Jesus with
Queen Victoria, for the queen dearly loved Jesus.
And Flo carefully explained what had gone wrong
at Scutari and how it was bound to happen again.

On one charming afternoon a shiny pony phae-
ton came rattling up the drive to Birk Hall; the
queen herself was out for a drive, all alone and
quite obviously enjoying herself. She walked in
the garden with Flo and stayed for tea.

She wagged her head. "Florence, Albert and I
cannot begin an action or appoint a royal commission. We can do that only after a cabinet minister advises us to do so."

"Secretary at War. Lord Panmure. I understand
he tends to put things off."

"Constantly. Pan thinks that if he ignores a problem it will eventually go away—or the government will change, and he needn't deal with it.
However, we'll call him up here, and you and I
can tackle him together. He will have a hard time
putting off a queen and a heroine both."

Did Flo succeed in charming Lord Panmure, Secretary at War? A few days later in a note, Sir John
Clark, Sir James's son, said, "You may like to know
that you fairly overcame Pan."

Her plan to change the army medical system
was on its way.

Now were you or I invited to a castle to visit one of the world's most famous queens we might just feel a wee bit nervous. But Flo was not you or I. Flo was used to meeting and greeting the very top of English society; queen, prince, duke, duchess, lord, and lady—and she was not the least afraid of them.

And that was one of the most extraordinary things about her; it made her an idol to the soldiers she served and a woman we admire today. The lady who could talk with royalty was genuinely concerned about every patient. A wounded soldier without family or friends still had one friend—the nurse at his bedside who called British lords by their first names. The millions of people in India, whom Flo would never meet, would soon become as important to her as her close family friends.

But—most important of all—she didn't just care. She put her care into action. She declined to marry the man she loved because it would have kept her from answering God's call. She risked her reputation to become a nurse. In Turkey she lost her health and worked under hideous conditions. In the years to come she would sacrifice her own wishes and comforts over and over again.

To help people she would never meet.

To ease more suffering than she could possibly imagine.

To save lives that were not yet born in her lifetime.

She was a friend of Queen Victoria.

But that's not why we remember Florence Nightingale. No. That's not why at all.

11

Death in the Barracks

Summer 1857

As Flo struggled to reform the army and its medical services so that the horror of Crimea would never happen again, far across the world tragedy was brewing. In exotic India, where wealthy maharajahs hunted tigers from the backs of elephants; where troops of monkeys romped among ruined temples; where tropical jungles lay at the feet of the world's highest, most dangerous mountains; Bengalese soldiers called Sepoys revolted against the British power there.

That Sepoy Rebellion changed the government of India; indeed, to this very day it affects the way Indians and British view each other. It sent thousands of British soldiers into an alien climate. And it brought sanitation in India to the attention of Florence Nightingale.

What we today call stress was already crushing her; it broke her fragile health and left her bedridden. But more, much more, was about to descend on her. Without leaving her rooms, she would soon become an expert on sanitary conditions of the British army in far-off India.

A royal commission investigated how the Crimean War had been conducted, with an eye to improvement. Two years later an India Sanitary Commission was put together, with an eye to saving the lives of troops in India. Once again, Flo found herself in the midst of it. For two years, people in India had been sending her information. Now she arranged all the facts and figures into charts and diagrams. She made the numbers tell her their secrets.

And the secrets were shocking.

The picture Flo saw was of a growing force of British soldiers sent to an alien land. The men who sent them knew nothing about that land, nor did the superior officers. Where most of the troops were sent, the winters were very warm, the summers exquisitely hot by English standards. Apparently local Indian men were hired for nearly all the everyday chores.

The reports told Flo of barracks built to house fifty men containing three hundred. Because native labor did most of the menial work, nothing at all remained for the soldiers to do save lie about. Water was considered pure if you couldn't actually see things floating in it. Supervisors seemed especially proud of their water if it didn't smell very bad. Privies? Drainage? Worse than Scutari! British soldiers sailed to India to die of disease, not bullets.

Neither were they strange and mysterious tropical diseases lurking in that foreign world. Cholera and other diseases found right in London were killing off Britain's troops in India.

When Flo superintended the hospital for Gentlewomen in Distressed Circumstances, someone —was it a Dr. Snow?—declared bad drinking water to be the carrier of cholera. That was more than fifteen years ago. At Scutari, cholera ended the moment the water supply and sewer system was cleaned up. Now the hard, cold numbers showed her the same diseases raging in the same filthy, crowded conditions a world away, in India.

She knew the answer, and it didn't matter how the question be framed; improve the drainage and water supply and troops would stop dying. So simple—and so difficult! Day by day she prepared work for the sanitary commission. And day by day she developed a master plan.

Just cleaning up the barracks would not really be enough, not so long as sickness was common a few yards away from the barracks. Soldiers would constantly bring disease back into their units from outside the grounds. India possessed great cities, true, but she was, like England, mostly a nation of villages. Begin with the villages. Teach the villagers how dangerous bad water and poor drainage are. Improve the lot of the villagers—prove the advantages of sanitation—and then move on to the cities (which require much costlier improvements than do small towns).

Again, Flo saw the vision. Again she must show others. And again she seemed to be the only one to see it. It was all *so* very discouraging!

Winter. Here it was again. How Flo hated the cold! Every year she seemed to tolerate it less. Even when she spent the whole winter, every day of it, inside these rooms at the Burlington, she didn't like it. The only bright spot—those few brief weeks of wishing everybody a happy Christmas —came and went.

The work remained. No matter how much she did, the work remained. No matter how many people came to visit, more remained to be seen. She drafted legislation that others would present in Parliament. She framed regulations to be adopted by the War Department. She wrote reports. She wrote letters by the thousand, words by the million. And she did it all from her sofa, usually with a cat draped around her shoulders.

In addition to all the work with the War Department, and the advice on hospitals she wrote to persons who asked, her training school was becoming a reality. That forty-five-thousand-pound Nightingale Fund she had felt to be such a burden? Now it was about to foot the bill for a training facility like no other.

At St. Thomas hospital, resident trainees would spend a year learning nursing. Each girl would have a room of her own, board, and ten pounds per year spending money. Each would attend lectures daily and keep a notebook (available for inspection on demand, lest the girl get a little lazy and let her notes fall behind). Each would attend chapel twice weekly. Girls would leave the building by twos, or not at all.

A year of study just to learn nursing? That was never done. Most nurses got the job first and learned as they went along. This could be very hard on patients, especially if some girl was a slow learner. Lectures? Chapel? Unheard of!

But Flo was creating a brand new nurse. Her new nurse would be a woman of high moral principles. Her new nurse would know her trade from the very start. Her new nurse would command respect; nursing would cease being a low-life trade. Flo's nurses would not be ordinary nurses. They would be expected to superintend nursing staffs and train other nurses. In short, they would be the best of the best.

It all sounded so good; and it all took so much work! Flo was house-ridden, and she might die at any time. Who would serve as matron? Who else could see the vision? How would they find and encourage the right kind of girls—upstanding young women who would love nursing the way Flo did?

She found her matron when the housemaid ushered Mrs. Wardroper into Flo's room. Mrs. Wardroper was square-built and solid. Her eye met Flo's and stayed there, firmly, confidently. She answered Flo's questions with a warm, easy-going voice.

"Mrs. Wardroper, when and how did you enter nursing?"

"My husband died when I was forty-two. I had children to support. The job paid enough to live on, for we're not extravagant, and I needed no training."

"You learned everything you know by experience only?"

"Most do. That's one reason I want this job so much. I think it's an evil that should be corrected. Mr. Whitefield, your associate in the school, told me your plans. I understand that the girls must hold high moral standards. I'm sure you have many enemies in this plan. They would pounce on any hint of sin and paint your whole school immoral; just as many people still think nursing is only for low, immoral women."

"Exactly. Mrs. Wardroper, we see the world through the same eyes. I look forward to a long, fruitful association with you."

A long, fruitful association? Oh, yes! Mrs. Wardroper served as the school matron for many years. She personally followed the progress of every student. So did Flo—every girl who enrolled. Together they adjusted the course work. Did girls need reading instruction? They received it. Poor spelling? Spelling drills. Medical and nursing skills? For a year they learned in the classroom and practiced in St. Thomas Hospital.

The image of the new nurse that Flo created during the Crimean War was now polished and multiplied. Only twenty-five suitable girls enrolled in the school's first year. The second year, there were more applicants than positions. Hospitals soon were begging for Nightingale nurses. The Nightingale School was a brilliant success.

A letter came in October from the former colonies. The Secretary of War in Washington, D.C., told of a growing conflict between the states. He asked her advice about organizing army hospitals and caring for sick and wounded. She sent him all the materials she thought might be useful. To a woman named Dorothea Dix, the superintendent of nurses in America, she sent her evidence presented to the commission in 1857. Miss Dix, as well as the secretary, should know about the good effects of well-prepared food, clean water supplies, and sanitation.

America's Civil War lasted four long years. During all those years, Flo kept up a lively correspondence with officials in the United States, offering advice and information. She helped shape medical policy in America.

Together with a wealthy man, Mr. Rathbone, Flo helped launch changes in the care of England's poor. A committed Christian, Mr. Rathbone used his vast wealth to reduce death and suffering among thousands of helpless poor people.

Flo worked for many years on the problem of sanitation in India. It would seem her grueling work was for nothing. But years later—for that is the way governments always work—the sanitary programs Flo recommended came at last to India.

Not only did the army make improvements, but local governments and the great cities as well. Drainage, sanitation, village education—Flo's vision became reality, and it promoted the good health of all people in India, just as she knew it could.

12

Red Crosses and Florence

July 1870

One of the reasons Papa had given Flo the little house on South Street was that South Street seemed such a quiet byway. Not today. Flo watched as wagons called field ambulances rattled by. Boxy, probably quite roomy inside, they looked more or less like delivery wagons. They were probably not very heavy; the teams of horses pulling them were fairly lightweight. Big crosses were painted on their sides.

Their purpose: to transport wounded men from the battlefield to the field hospitals. Their destination: the border between France and Germany.

For France and Germany were threatening each other with war, and Flo was torn. Some of her best friends were German, others were French. Kaiserwerth was in Germany. Once upon a time Germany had been a center of scientific advance. Now most of Germany was called Prussia, a military state, thundering and proud. Flo didn't like the change; she hated the war.

"Sir Harry Verney, Miss Nightingale."

"Show him in." Flo arranged her lace collar and dumped the cat in her lap off onto the floor. It hopped right back up onto her sofa and curled into a warm, furry ball at her feet.

Flo's brother-in-law's hair was whiter, his eagle nose a bit more pointed, but he hadn't changed much. "Flo, and good day! Parthe sends her love." He drew up a chair and plopped it down close before her. "I've an immense favor to ask of you."

"I suspect the answer is no, but ask away."

He sat back and laced his fingers together. "Several of us are establishing an aid society. It's official name is the National Society for Aid to the Sick and Wounded. British Red Cross Aid Society. I'm on its executive committee. So are Douglas Galton and my daughter Emily."

"Its purpose?"

"To step in and render aid where aid is lacking. Like what you did at Scutari. Being a private organization, we can act promptly when government agencies are bogged down."

"I'm not sure you—any of you—realize what you're committed to. Those who undertake the work of aiding the sick and wounded must not be sentimental enthusiasts, but downright lovers of hard work. It was a dismal, grinding struggle with a thousand details to be corrected one by one. No honor, no glory, no romance."

He smiled. "I'm sure you're right; you've been there. The favor we ask is that you take control of the society and direct it—precisely because you *have* been there. You know what must be done and how to do it. And you have a genius for organization."

"I'm flattered." Flo thought, but she didn't have to think long. "I'm sorry, Harry. Take control? I can't. It would consume too much of my time. I spend many hours every day on the Indian sanitation problem."

"I thought that suffered a set-back."

"It did. Douglas and I made certain strong recommendations about barracks construction. The Royal Engineers ignored our plans and went with their own. Took none of our suggestions. Dismal failure, but the sanitary commission took the blame. Still, we've all spent far too much time and effort for me to turn my back on the project now. No. I'm sorry."

"Mm." The eagle brow puckered. "Our primary concern at the moment, of course, is the possible war between France and Prussia. We're sending observers over. They need someone on this side of the channel who can receive their reports and act on them. Will you do that for us?"

"How can I refuse?"

In a frightening way it was much like the Crimea all over again. On August second—nine years to the day since Sidney Herbert died, Flo noted— the French drove the Germans out of the town of Saarebruck. The war was on.

Flo sent notes around to a few friends and brought the Red Cross Society five thousand pounds in donations in one week. The society sent her cousin

Henry Bonham Carter and her old doctor John Sutherland to the front lines in France as observers. They sent back horror stories about French army inefficiency.

In the Crimean War sixteen years ago, French medical services had been excellent, far superior to the British. Now here were the French floundering in red tape as men died—the same tune played on new pipes. An eerie feeling overtook Flo, that this had all happened before.

As she read John's reports of disease, the sweet-sour stench of cholera came strong to her mind. Henry's bulletins brought her vivid pictures of blood and filth and amputations, gangrenous limbs and torn flesh. With the lamp of imagination she walked the corridors of her memories. Behind her on the walls, silent shadows swarmed again.

Her dead. Her nine thousand dead in the pits of Scutari.

And yet, there was a profound difference this time. Again she found herself writing pages and pages of advice. But this time people heeded her advice. Again she interviewed hospital volunteers and sent them off, but this time they were gladly received. She supervised purchases and sent supplies, and no one opposed her or objected. Just like the old days, when something needed doing, "ask Miss Nightingale." Flo felt like an old war horse with the smell of new battle in its nostrils.

Mercifully, the war lasted less than six months.

In 1872 the concept of the British Red Cross Aid Society expanded world-wide; a Swiss banker named Jean Henry Dunant brought about the Geneva Convention and founded the International Red Cross. In London he read a paper explaining the work of the society.

It began: "Though I am known as the founder of the Red Cross, and the originator of the convention of Geneva, it is to an Englishwoman that all the honor of that convention is due. What inspired me . . . was the work of Miss Florence Nightingale in the Crimea."

13

Jubilee

April 1880

Why should the iron wheel of that gardener's hand barrow be so wide? From her bedroom window Flo watched him push the barrow up into the tilled soil of a flower bed. That was why; so it wouldn't sink in soft dirt. Briskly, he began burying, one by one, the gray tubers in his barrow. Dahlias. The summer's bloom.

Flo saw the last of the crocus there, and the hyacinth buds just starting. Were they blooming wild in the Crimea this year? Yellow jonquils and deep blue muscari—the present—splashed lovely color across the Dorchester House Gardens even as the gardener was busying himself planting the future.

"Mum? A Charles Gordon to see you."

"Thank you." Flo held out a hand. She let her maid help her down the stairs. She settled herself on her sofa, covered her legs with a shawl, and nodded. The maid showed him in.

What a dashing man! You took one look at him and felt instantly inclined to follow whatever orders he might give.

He gave none. With a gracious bow he kissed her hand. "I was twenty-one when I sailed away from home to serve in the Crimea. My dream then has finally come true—to meet the legend who saved so many lives. God bless you richly, Miss Nightingale!"

"You're a legend in your own right, Chinese Gordon. I'm honored by your visit. Do be seated." She motioned for tea.

She tried to picture him in a fez; in the Sudan, she knew, he had worn one; but he looked much too British. "I've long admired your enlightened attitude, particularly the way you care about the people of India."

"I know a little something of your efforts for sanitation in India." He studied her with clear blue-gray eyes. "You look sad."

She tried to smile, but there was nothing worth smiling about. "These last eight years have been the hardest of my life. Worse than the lowest points of my youth. Worse even than the Crimea. I had to give up several worthy projects because I had to spend my time and efforts managing the family estates. Two years I spent thus. I thought I was miserable then.

"Six years ago my father died falling down a flight of stairs he'd been climbing for thirty years. Mother was ill; my sister refused to take her. So did Mama's brothers and sisters."

Flo sighed, the wounds still so fresh. "Mama died two months ago, at ninety-two. During her long lingering, I lost my contacts with the War Office. When I asked for some facts and figures from the India Office two years ago they refused my request. Now that I'm free again to work, I've no job to do. There was a day when I could recommend an appointment and it was made. No more."

He studied her thoughtfully with those penetrating eyes. "Then I believe I have some good news for you. You have a friend, I believe, a Lord de Grey."

"Lord de Grey's been elevated; he is Lord Ripon now. Yes."

"I'm sure you know that in the election just held, the Liberals won. Your Lord Ripon is about to become Viceroy to India. If that's not a foot in the India Office door, what is?"

Flo's heart fluttered, but it wasn't her old malady. It was a tiny bird of hope, beating its wings deep inside her.

He leaned forward. "The reason I came, Miss Nightingale: my cousin, Mrs. Hawthorn, gave the War Office information about the bad treatment and neglect rendered by orderlies in military hospitals. Horror stories. They don't believe her. We feel if anyone can bring the matter to bear, you can."

"Prime Minister Gladstone's ministers and I do not get on. But I'll see what I can do. I'll need all her facts and figures—everything. I must work from facts."

The tea arrived. Conversation turned to religion. Flo had heard that Charles George Gordon

was a religious man, and it pleased her immense-
ly that his view of the fruits of religion agreed
with hers. The fruit of union with God was practi-
cal good works. Here was true religion—don't tell
God you revere Him, prove it!

A month later he gave Flo a little book of religious writings and sailed to India as Lord de Grey/
Ripon's secretary.

So Flo was in it again. It took her two years to
get Mrs. Hawthorne's information confirmed and
a committee of inquiry launched. By October she
was drawing graphs and preparing witnesses, sending briefs—the old war horse again taking up the
battle against mismanagement—and she loved it!

Lord Ripon knew where to get information about
Indian affairs, too. Flo's mountains of papers and
reports had become Himalayas of papers and reports. Reports the India Office had lost twenty
years before were still in her records. Flo became,
in effect, the India Office's historical records li-
brary, dispensing the facts and figures she loved
so well.

A busy life again, and no family duties—Flo had
never been happier. She kept contact as Colonel
Gordon became General Gordon and traveled
from India to China to Basutoland in Africa (she
had to look that one up) and the Cape of Good
Hope.

In 1884 General Gordon went to the Sudan to
put down a rebellion and was besieged at Khartoum. Flo followed the reports closely as the War
Office sent a relief expedition (they certainly took
their sweet time about it!). Included in the expedi-

tion was a unit of female army nurses, officially requested. Ah, but Flo liked that! Her nurses were in demand by the army itself. Once upon a time, Flo fought bitterly for army nursing. The War Office was finally realizing their worth.

One dispatch reported that a party of nurses had been sent up the Nile to Wadi Halfa. Wadi Halfa. Thirty-four years before, Flo herself had gone up to the Nile to Wadi Halfa, on that extended tour of Egypt with Charles and Sigma. How miserably unhappy she had been then. And why? Because she heard God's call to nursing and feared she would never succeed in that call. And now . . .

On January 26, after nearly a year of fighting, the rebels besieging Khartoum overwhelmed its defenders. The city fell. With savage fury the rebels massacred every British soldier and sympathizer in it.

Two days later—two days too late—the Gordon Relief Expedition arrived.

Flo felt an overwhelming sense of loss. Yet she knew that whether man should win or lose, succeed or fail, God was in control. It had taken her a lifetime to understand that.

General Gordon had donated much of his salary and efforts to homeless boys. When in his memory the Gordon Home for Destitute Boys was founded, Flo took an active part in it.

Richard Monckton Milnes died.

What would it have been like, being Mrs. Monckton Milnes? She still wondered sometimes.

In 1897 Queen Victoria celebrated her Diamond Jubilee, sixty years on the throne. Flo observed her own private little jubilee; it was exactly sixty years since she first heard God call her to His service.

One morning in March, when the weather was nasty, a Lady Wantage came calling. Flo was nearly blind now, but she could tell that this woman looked much like Sigma, or perhaps Liz Herbert—beautiful, sophisticated, charming. Lady Wantage was out collecting mementos for a glorious Victoria Era Exhibition. Florence Nightingale and the growth of trained nursing would surely be one of its most popular displays. Might Miss Nightingale please provide some mementos of herself. Some relics of the Crimean War?

Flo snorted. "Relics of the Crimean War? They are first the tremendous lessons we have had to learn from its tremendous blunders and ignorances. And next they are the trained nurses and the progress of hygiene."

But Lady Wantage would not be put off by facts and lessons. "You still advise the War Office on some matters, is that true?"

"Yes." Flo must be wary; here was a sharp one.

"And the India Office seeks your advice, I understand."

"They're making splendid progress in sanitation, you know. The great cities are drained by sewers now—Madras especially. And the Bombay Village Sanitation Act brought cleanliness to the villages —what I've been preaching all along. And—"

"Yes! Yes, Miss Nightingale. Don't you see? Men of power still value your opinion. The Queen wants to honor you as a servant of God who is still serving. You are the era!"

And that smooth-talking, lovely woman wangled from Flo her few mementos of her life of service. When the Diamond Jubilee Victorian Era Exhibition opened, right in the center of the Florence Nightingale-and-nursing exhibit stood *the dead-axle baggage cart from Balaclava.*

In the late 1980s in America, hospitals suffered a shortage of nurses. So they brought some British nurses over to relieve the shortage, because British nurses are among the best trained in the world. Now how do you suppose that started?!

On May 10, 1907, the Nightingale Training School celebrated its own jubilee. By its hundredth birthday there were more than a thousand nurses' training schools in the United States alone.

Her sanitary improvements, begun in India, have spread around the world to nearly all countries. Cholera is rare today.

And the lady who's life work helped all this happen? Like her mother, she went blind in her old age. And like her mother, she lost the ability to understand what was going on around her.

By February of 1910, she no longer spoke. She lay quietly in her bed with her hands folded, resting at long last after a lifetime of illness and frustrating work. On August 13, 1910, she fell asleep about noon. She did not wake again.

Epilogue

And now I've one last question for you: Where is Florence Nightingale today?

"Why," you insist, "in heaven with God. She did all those good things!"

Flo did work hard and suffer much; she was certain she was doing God's will. She accomplished wonderful things for soldiers and thousands of others. But doing good can't get people into heaven, and Flo couldn't buy her way to heaven with good deeds any more than you can. Knowing Jesus is the only way to heaven.

Only what Jesus did can get us into heaven. Jesus' suffering and death paid for my sin, your sin, and Flo's sin (oh, yes; everyone has sinned, even Flo). When we accept Jesus' payment, the Bible says, we become His. Then, you see, because He did so very much for us, we gladly give Him our service. He wants the good things we do to show that we're *already* safe, heaven-bound.

Did Flo know Jesus? Did she realize how much He did for her? We don't know. And that is the answer to my last question: we simply don't know. But what a loss it would be if she did so much, only to miss out on the one thing every person must do—give oneself to Jesus!

How about you?

FLORENCE NIGHTINGALE'S LIFE

A Chronology

May 12, 1820	Florence born in Florence, Italy. Her sister Parthenope (b. in Naples) is a year old.
1825	Papa William Edward Nightingale buys Embley near Romsey, in England, as their winter home.
September 1837	Flo perceives a call from God but doesn't know how she is to serve Him. The Nightingales embark on a European tour while Embley is being remodeled. Return to England, 1839.
March 1840	Aunt Mai tries to arrange math lessons for Flo; Mama thwarts them. Ladies don't need math.

May 1842	Flo meets Richard Monckton Milnes. Flo is attracted but resists his attentions.
Winter 1843-44	Aunt Hannah Nicholson enlarges Flo's spiritual horizons.
December 1845	Flo wants to work and train at Salisbury Infirmary nearby. Because of the reputation of nursing in that day, Mama and Parthe are horrified. A cultured lady of that day did not enter into hospital work.
1846	Lord Ashley tells her about the government reports called Blue Books. She becomes a self-taught expert on hospitals and sanitation.
Spring 1847	She is approaching a mental breakdown. Sigma and Charles Bracebridge rescue her by taking her to Rome with them. There she meets Sidney and Liz Herbert.
June 1848	Flo attends opening of Herbert's Charmouth convalescent home, and her expertise is recognized.
1849	Richard Monckton Milnes demands a yes or no to his marriage proposal. Heartbroken, Flo says no. Marriage would destroy her chance of serving God's call.

1849-50	Flo accompanies the Bracebridges to Egypt and Greece, again for respite from strain at home. She is frustrated, driven by her call, unable to train or serve.
August 1851	She is allowed to train at Kaiserwerth in Germany. She claims she received no nursing training there, but learned discipline and administration.
April 1853	She heads Institution for the Care of Sick Gentlewomen in Distressed Circumstances.
August 12, 1853	She begins work on Harley St., learning a little nursing and a lot of administration—making do with nothing.
October 1854	Sidney Herbert calls her to Crimea with thirty-eight women nurses. This is her opportunity, her grand experiment, to show the value of female nurses in military hospitals. Assured of abundant supplies and splendid facilities, her nurses walk into horror. There is nothing. Doctors' resistance is broken down by the sheer enormity of the calamity. Flo emerges a heroine to the troops.

July 16, 1856	The last patients leave Scutari hospital. Flo goes home.
1856	Obsessed with a need to correct abuses that caused the Crimean calamity, Flo meets Queen Victoria, arranges a royal commission to investigate the system. Flo invents new ways to express figures in graph form. Using graphs and tables to "sell" an idea such as sanitation had never before been done the way she did it. It is common practice now.
Summer 1857	The Sepoy Rebellion in India. Flo becomes wrapped up in what will be a life-long interest: sanitation in India. Not until very late in her life, however, will her reforms be put into practice, and then by others.
June 1860	The Nightingale Training School for nurses opens at St. Thomas Infirmary with Mrs. Wardroper as its head. The school is a brilliant success; Flo almost single-handedly forges the modern image of the competent, moral, noble nurse.
August 2, 1861	Army officials in America ask her advice on care of sick and wounded in U.S. Civil War. She sends

information to Secretary of War and Dorothea Dix, Superintendent of Nurses.

William Rathbone asks her help in setting up a home nurse system in Liverpool. She cannot provide direct help, but advises.

1864	William Rathbone comes asking for matron and nurses for Liverpool Workhouse Infirmary. Cost of patient care goes down.
January 1865	Flo becomes involved in poor law reform. A partial enactment of her suggestions in 1867 will be basis of later reforms.
July 1870	Flo advises the British Red Cross Society.
August 1874	Father dies by accident. For six years Flo will tend her mother while she chafes and aches to get back to her real work and calling. They are the most difficult years of her life.
	William Rathbone asks her help in establishing home nursing in London. She cannot because of Mama, but she advises. With her guidance he puts reform through —plan is a great success.
February 2, 1880	Fanny Nightingale, Flo's mama, dies, blind and senile. Flo gets

	back into War Office and Indian affairs in time to see nurses used and progress made, both in reform and in attitudes.
February 1894	Flo is now going blind.
June 1897	Queen Victoria's Diamond Jubilee. Victorian Age Exhibition opens. Flo is honored.
1907	The Order of Merit is bestowed on her.
August 13, 1910	She dies quietly in her sleep.